E. A Judges

In and Around Guildford

Old and New

E. A Judges

In and Around Guildford
Old and New

ISBN/EAN: 9783337193515

Printed in Europe, USA, Canada, Australia, Japan

Cover: Foto ©Andreas Hilbeck / pixelio.de

More available books at **www.hansebooks.com**

In and Around Guildford:

Old and New. By E. A. Judges.

With nearly Seventy Illustrations.

Guildford:
'Surrey Times' Office.
MDCCCXCV.

CONTENTS.

—◆◆—

CHAPTER I.

THE HIGH STREET : PAST AND PRESENT.

CHAPTER II.

GUILDFORD CASTLE AND THE ROYAL MANOR.

CHAPTER III.

THE TOWN HALL.

CHAPTER IV.

THE ONSLOWS.

CHAPTER V.

THE FRIARY.

CHAPTER VI.

ARCHBISHOP ABBOT.

CHAPTER VII.

THE ROYAL GRAMMAR SCHOOL.

CHAPTER VIII.

THE RUSSELLS.

CHAPTER IX.

THE TOWN CHURCHES.

CHAPTER X.

ST. CATHERINE'S, LOSELEY, AND COMPTON.

CHAPTER XI.

MERROW, SHERE, ALBURY, ST. MARTHA'S, AND SHALFORD.

LIST OF ILLUSTRATIONS.

[Except where otherwise stated, the plates are produced from photographs especially taken by Mr. W. Shawcross, Spital Street, Guildford.]

FRONTISPIECE.

The Old Corn Market, Guildford. *From a print dated 1819, in the possession of Lord Ashcombe*

CHAPTER I.

THE HIGH STREET.

CHAPTER II.

THE CASTLE.

CHAPTER III.

THE TOWN HALL.

CHAPTER IV.
THE ONSLOWS.

CHAPTER V.
THE FRIARY.

CHAPTER VI.
ARCHBISHOP ABBOT.

CHAPTER VII.
THE GRAMMAR SCHOOL.

CHAPTER VIII.
THE RUSSELLS.

* The illustrations in this chapter are reproduced by kind permission of Mr. G. C. Williamson from his " Life of Russell " (G. Bell and Sons).

CHAPTER IX.

THE TOWN CHURCHES.

CHAPTER X.

ST. CATHERINE'S, LOSELEY, AND COMPTON.

CHAPTER XI.

MERROW, SHERE, ALBURY, ST. MARTHA'S, AND SHALFORD.

INTRODUCTION.

JUST fifty years have elapsed since the publication of the last edition of Russell's " History of Guildford." During that period no attempt has been made to place before those who know and love the old town any permanent record or review of its many features of picturesque and archæological interest.

The following pages will, it is hoped, in some slight degree make good this omission. They do not, however, purport to be in any sense a history of the borough. The work Russell first set on foot a century ago will, I trust, one day be carried on with all the completeness which antiquarian knowledge and recent research can give ; Mr. G. C. Williamson, as is well known, has long been collecting materials for this task, which will be to him essentially a labour of love. My aim has been different and far simpler. I have refrained from touching upon much that would appeal to the antiquary and the archæologist, and have omitted much that it would be needful to include in any exhaustive chronicle of Guildford's past. I have simply striven to examine a few chapters in our local annals ; to tell a part only of what may be told of the chief events and personages prominent in these records ; and to suggest the extent of, rather than to exhaust, the wealth of interesting associations and natural attractions to which the town and its neighbourhood can justly lay claim.

I trust, nevertheless, that the present volume will be found to contain no small store of information of local value not otherwise easily accessible. Since Russell's time material additions have been made to the knowledge of our municipal history ; of the traditions and memories linked with the High Street, the Castle, the Friary, and the Grammar School ; and of the careers and characters of Guildfordians, who, like George Abbot, Arthur Onslow, and John Russell, have won their way to fame. I have tried to profit in some degree by the labours which have given us this truer and fuller view of the past, and to weave the facts so gathered into a concise and intelligible narrative.

In almost all cases my indebtedness to the authorities thus appealed to is acknowledged in the text. But it is only right to mention here, that in addition to Russell's publications and the standard county histories, I have had recourse to the invaluable works of Mr. G. T. Clark on " Mediæval Military Architecture," and of Dr. Grose on " The Gild Merchant "; to papers by Mr. D. M. Stevens and others in the collections of the Surrey Archæological Society ; to Mr. G. C. Williamson's " Life of John Russell "; to the " Notes and Queries " which for some while appeared in the *Surrey Times :* to Mr. J. Cordy Jeaffreson's catalogue of the Loseley MSS. ; to Mr. Palmer's " Memorials of Holy Trinity Church "; and to Mr. Whitburn's lectures on the town pictures. etc.

The recent improvements in the methods of " process " reproduction enable absolutely faithful views of scenes and buildings to be given with an accuracy and an artistic finish which a few years ago were quite unattainable. These will, I believe, add materially to the permanent value of the volume.

I have to tender very hearty thanks to the Earl of Onslow, Lord Ashcombe, Sir Charles H. Stuart Rich, Bart., Mr. G. F. Watts, R.A., and Mr. W. More-Molyneux for the generous kindness with which they have placed books and documents, old prints and photographs at my service, or have allowed photographs to be taken.

Similar help has also been given with equal readiness by Mr. Williamson, who has, in addition, allowed me to include several illustrations of special local interest from his biography of John Russell, and to reproduce for this volume the valuable and noteworthy portrait of Archbishop Abbot now in his possession.

Mr. T. M. Brownrigg has specially favoured me by permitting the reproduction of several of his exquisite photographic views of scenes in and near the town : and Mr. G. J. Jacobs and Mr. A E. Moon have kindly shown me the same courtesy in respect of views of the Castle, the Grammar School, Loseley Chapel, Shalford Church, etc. Messrs. Stent and Sons have most willingly granted the use of several of the woodcuts originally made for the 1845 edition of Russell's " History of Guildford." The views of St. Catherine's and St. Martha's Chapels are reproduced by arrangement with Messrs. Poulton and Sons.

In all other cases the illustrations are from photographs specially executed for this work by Mr. W. Shawcross of Guildford, who has throughout spared neither time nor pains to give me the full benefit of his professional skill and experience.

I may, perhaps, add that the preparation of the book in the scanty leisure of the past year has afforded much real pleasure to one who, although not a Guildfordian by birth, yields to none in his affection for the town, or in the sincerity of his desire that its future may not be less happy or prosperous than its past.

                                                          E. A. J.

IN AND AROUND GUILDFORD:

OLD AND NEW.

CHAPTER I.

THE HIGH STREET: PAST AND PRESENT.

HERE is no gainsaying the fact that the townspeople of Guildford point to the High Street with unabashed pride. Perhaps it may not fully merit the praise bestowed upon it by one authority when he termed it "the prettiest in the South of England." Yet who will deny that it can boast of charms, not lightly to be assessed, in the quaint gables, the overhanging windows, the panelled fronts, and the picturesque glimpses across the valley to the ridge beyond, which attract the eye as we descend the steep hill towards the eastern banks of the Wey? Who can wonder that a High Street so rich in varied beauty wins the admiration of the passing visitor, and the lasting affection of all to whom the town is "Home," and its records therefore dear?

The street is, of course, and always has been, the heart of the borough, old and new. If we could trace in detail the changing scenes its bricks and stones have witnessed, we should know almost all that need be known of Guildford's past. For, inevitably, much of our local history centres round the Town Hall, the red-brick Church and its predecessor at the top of the hill, Trinity Hospital opposite, and the Grammar School a few yards further on. Here assuredly, if anywhere, Guildford's traditions must cluster and linger. Scarce a house can be passed, or a foot of ground trodden, which cannot claim some interesting link with bygone days. But of this vanished past there is much that neither pen nor pencil can now recall. And as my purpose is to refer in a later page to the story which Town Hall and Church,

1

Hospital and Grammar School, alike have to tell, I must content myself now with offering a few notes upon some of the characteristics the old street has presented at different stages of its history, and upon some memorable incidents of which it has been the scene.

Deferring for the present all question as to earlier settlements on the opposite river bank, it is difficult to say how and when High Street first began to cover the hillside. Mr. T. G. Clark, in his "Mediæval Architecture," suggests that it certainly existed in the thirteenth century, and probably some centuries before. Possibly its development was aided by the "local greed for building material," to which the same writer in part attributes the decay of the Castle. Or there may be good ground for the hint thrown out by other inquirers, that the chalk dug from the caverns under Quarry Hill was largely used for building purposes in the chief street when the town was yet young. But concerning these points we must be content to guess, and we must start much nearer our own times in a hasty glance at the more recent past.

The first well-defined picture of the street which can now be conceived dates back, indeed, only some two or three centuries. In Elizabethan times, as probably earlier still, it was essentially, and above all, a market street, in which the whole trade of the town and neighbourhood centred. It was here that the farmers and the corn-factors, the vendors of cattle, sheep, pigs, poultry, and fish, the dealers in "shoes, gloves, bucketts, bowls, crocks, dishes," and every other household requisite, had their recognised station, and week by week carried on their transactions.

First as to the Corn Market. It "acquired importance," says Russell somewhat vaguely, "at a very early period." Originally, the weekly sale on Saturday was held beneath the Guildhall. But an old memorandum tells us that, in 1625, "whereas the marketts of this towne of late years (thanks be to God) have much increased, and by order and care thereunto had are dailie like to be greater and greater," and whereas the market-house, "by reason of a multitude of corne brought to be sold there hath not bene nor is sufficient to contain the wheate, barleye, pease, and other grayne accustimablie sold there," the Mayor and his colleagues built a new wheat market-house on the west of the Tunn Inn. This building, of which a representation is given in the frontispiece, is described in a footnote to Russell's "History" (1845 edition) as "merely a niche in the basement of the Tunn Inn, widened by a flattened roof to the extent of the footway, where the same was supported by some wooden columns. This roof formed an advantageous balcony to the Inn. At the back of this there existed, about thirty years ago, large warehouses for wool."

HIGH STREET, LOOKING EAST.

Poor though this improved accommodation was, it met all requirements till 1818, when the "present chaste and commodious structure"—such was Russell's phrase—was erected. Its cost, including the site, was nearly £4,700, of which the Corporation provided £2,500, and the balance was subscribed by the inhabitants and their neighbours. For years the room in the rear was used as the Criminal Court during the Assizes, civil causes being heard in the Guild Hall. In return, a portion of the latter building was at one time taken advantage of for storing wheat when the supply was unusually large.

But to turn back to the High Street of Elizabethan days. In 1578 the present open space in front of Holy Trinity Church was utilized by Thomas Baker, a clothier, for providing an erection, known as Baker's Market-House, for the sale of rye, malt, and oats, and used also as a school, for "the teaching of the poor men's children of the town to write and read English, and to cast accompte." This market-house was a clumsy erection, built entirely of wood, with a dwelling-house attached. But not until 1758 was its destruction finally resolved upon, and an octagonal

BAKER'S MARKET HOUSE.
(Originally drawn for the " History of Guildford, 1845 Edition, published by Messrs. G. W. and J. Russell.)

building of brick and stone put up in its place. For many years after 1758 the school was held in the tower of Trinity Church, but later on it was amalgamated with another charity left by Archbishop Abbot, and Abbot's School was founded.

The Cattle Market held sway in High Street on Tuesdays, until its removal, in 1865, to North Street, now happily about to be forsaken for a site in Woodbridge Road ; and century after century a brisk trade in pigs was on Saturday carried on beneath the shadow of Abbot's Hospital. Just opposite Swan Lane the Shambles adorned the thoroughfare till 1685, when they were pulled down and rebuilt by the Corporation on a plot of ground which still bears that name. In front of the Angel Inn was the Fyshe Crosse, till, in 1593, a wooden house was erected on the same spot to serve as the fish market. The poultry market was held, until 1592, between the Tun and the White Hart Inns ; thence it was removed to the space between the Lion and the George Inns, and finally to a building, known and used as the cockpit, next to the Theatre in Market Street. For this market, as well as for those for vegetables and butcher's meat—as, in turn, they had been driven from the High Street—accommodation was provided in the building which was erected in 1789 in

Market Street, by Lords Grantley and Onslow, as the Sessions House and the Assize Court, and which was also the scene of the Corporation feasts, and of much of the ordinary business and amusements of the town.

Even thus, however, we have not quite exhausted the list of vendors for whom space was found in High Street three centuries ago. Dealers in oatmeal and bread were arrayed against the Crown Inn, now Mr. Vickridge's premises ; shoemakers and glovers stood eastward of the Round House, on the south side of the street ; "bucketts, bowles, crocks, dishes, or other vessells made of wood or earth," were given a similar location ; and the tanners had their stands from the South Lane, commonly called the lane at Ravell's Corner, also on the south side of the thoroughfare. A busy scene, doubtless, but a strange medley the street, as it was in those good old days, would present to modern eyes.

Another characteristic feature must not be forgotten. The town authorities were resolved to secure "bold advertisement" for what was then the staple industry of the place. An order was made in 1575 that every alehouse keeper should have a signboard, with a wool-sack painted on it, hung up at his door under a penalty of 6s. 8d. for neglect. Guildford cloth, indeed, had won no little fame for the town. For the wool-pack, tightly tied by the corners, had been added to the town arms by special permission of the Merchants of the Staple, the chief guild of traders in wool. But neither this notable recognition of merit nor the advertising alertness of the Corporation sufficed to enable Guildford to retain pre-eminence in the trade. By slow degrees the supremacy at one time enjoyed was lost, and though Archbishop Abbot twice strove, as we shall presently see, to bring about a revival of the industry, his efforts were futile.

High Street, however, was not allowed to lose its brightness. A plentiful display of gaudily-painted trade signs of various kinds was maintained long after Elizabeth's time. These signs must often have attracted the notice of travellers who, in the old stage-coach and posting days—when, by the bye, the unwary pedestrian was often deluged by the streaming water-spouts which projected from every dwelling—found the town, with its numerous hostelries, a convenient halting-place. Pepys more than once illustrates this fact in his gossiping pages. Thus, to quote only one or two entries :

"1662, 22nd of April. We came to Gilford, and there passed our time in the garden cutting up asparagus for supper, the best that ever I eat in my life, but in this house last year."

"1668, 6th of August. Away to Gilford, losing our way three or four miles about Cobham. At Gilford we dined, and I showed them the Hospitall there of Bishop Abbot and his tomb in the Church, which with the rest of the tombs there are kept mighty clean and neat with curtains before them. So to coach again and on to Liphook."

"1688, August 7. Came at night to Gilford, where the Red Lion was so full of people and a wedding that the master of the house did get us a lodging over the way, at a private house, his landlord's, mighty neat and fine."

Local publications, dating back only some sixty years, furnish particulars of the coaching service through the town, which amply suffice to suggest how this busy traffic both brightened and profited the High Street. Thus, as lately as in 1836, at a time when the townspeople were first meeting to consider the expediency of a railroad, and decided to make inquiries thereon, nineteen

THE OLD BRIDGE.
(*From a print in the "Gentleman's Magazine," 1754.*)

coaches regularly passed through the town. Fourteen served Southampton, Portsmouth, and London : two London and Chichester : and one London and Littlehampton ; while a cross-country service was kept up between Brighton and Oxford, and Brighton and Windsor. Some of the approaches to the town, however, it must be confessed, were not free from drawbacks. Before very desirable improvements were made by the construction of the roads now used, many complaints were heard of the narrowness and steepness of Bury Street, along which the old Portsmouth Road was formerly continued to the foot of the Old Bridge, and of the terribly stiff climb required to reach the Hog's Back viâ The Mount and the old Farnham Road. One reminiscence of these times must not be overlooked. It was no strange sight, we are told, for large batches of convicts, brought by road from Portsmouth, to pass through Guildford heavily

laden with chains ; while, in time of war, a sad and pathetic scene was sometimes witnessed as the wounded, on their homeward journey, changed vehicles
opposite Holy Trinity Church. The Star Corner, I may add, was the
rendezvous of most of the country carriers, and for some at least of the
"errand men and women" who helped to keep up communication with the
adjacent villages.

As in many another town, the High Street still retains, in the number of
its inns, one obvious relic of coaching days. To one or two of these houses
interesting associations belong. The Angel, for example, carries us back to the
time when on the same site stood the hostel of the Carmelites or White Friars,
from which, as dedicated to St. Michael and All Angels, the inn most probably
derives its name. Of this religious house, indeed, we know nothing save its
dedication and position "hard by the
Fysshe House." Some chantries were
attached to it, and the existence of the
hostel possibly explains the origin of the
two crypts which may still be seen beneath
the Angel and the house opposite.

Higher up the hill the White Hart
and the Crown at one time faced one
another as respectively the recognised
headquarters of the two great political
parties. The Crown has for some years
ceased to be a licensed house ; but from
its windows, and from those of the White
Hart, many a stirring speech has been
delivered, and in the roadway beneath
many a lively election episode occurred.

Equally memorable, and far more
discreditable, were the "Guy Riots," which
for years disturbed and disgraced the town,
and especially the High Street, as the
5th of November recurred. For generations the "young bloods" of Guildford
were not content with a peaceable, if noisy, demonstration of their loyalty.
Year after year they ruthlessly damaged property, inflicted injury, and
endangered life. Matters reached a climax early in the sixties of the present
century. On the Prince of Wales's wedding-day (March 10, 1863) the
Guys turned out in force. According to custom, they marched through the
streets in military fashion, bearing lighted torches and bundles of chips and

THE CROWN INN, NOW OCCUPIED BY MR.
VICKRIDGE.
(Originally drawn for Russell's "History of Guildford.")

faggots, arrayed in grotesque costumes, and armed with formidable bludgeons, three feet long, studded with square nails. They pulled down palings, broke windows, and generally disported themselves without regard to the life or limbs of those around them. And finally they kindled a huge bonfire on their "old spot" in front of Holy Trinity Church. In November of the same year a considerable detachment of troops, both foot and horse, from Aldershot, was billeted in the town, and 600 special constables were sworn in as extraordinary precautions to ensure order. The fifth, in consequence, passed off quietly. But on the 21st of the month, immediately after the departure of the military, the Guys were in evidence again. Though fewer in number than of yore, they attacked and partially demolished the houses of two of the borough magistrates. But this was almost their last escapade. Strong measures were taken by the town authorities, and, thanks to the determination of the then Mayor, Mr. W. Jacob, and the Superintendent of Police, Mr. John Law, peace

OLD HOUSES IN HIGH STREET.
(Originally drawn for Russell's " History of Guildford.")

and order in the long run triumphed. One serious encounter took place ; the Guys were completely routed, three or four of their number were captured, and afterwards sentenced to imprisonment.

Centuries before, popular pastimes of a less violent character were annually indulged in in High Street with the full sanction and concurrence of the community. In the Middle Ages, Guildfordians in each year chose a Summer King and two satellites, known as the Prince and Sword-bearer, who presided over the sports of May Day and Whitsuntide. And it is significant that in Henry VIII.'s time it was ordered that a penalty of 5s. should be imposed on anyone who refused to serve the office of King, and a fine of 2s. 3d. and 1s. 8d. respectively in the case of the Prince and the Sword-bearer. These sums, it may be mentioned, were to be paid to the churches of which the offenders were parishioners. How long the custom was maintained it is impossible to say. But the Summer Pole, which for years had stood opposite St. Mary's Church, was ordered to be taken down in 1610-1611 by the general consent of the Mayor and his brethren. More fortunate was the May pole, which retained

2

its position at the top of Spital Street, by the junction of the Epsom and the London Roads, till early in the present century. On the other hand, the fact, alas! has to be recorded that as recently as 1820 the brutal punishment of flogging at the cart's tail was witnessed in the High Street. The last local victim of this inhuman treatment was dragged thus from the Angel to the Red Lion Inn, while the Town Crier, in the presence of a huge crowd, vigorously applied the cat.

To-day High Street seems to many visitors to merge somewhat arbitrarily into Spital Street. A century ago Duke Street was the eastward continuation of the main thoroughfare, and led to Stoke-above-Bars. Duke Street obviously owed its name to Somerset House, which may still be seen close by the Grammar School, and which was erected early last century by the Duke of Somerset, to obviate the necessity of sleeping at an inn in the town on his frequent journeys to and from Petworth. The designation of Spital Street is, however, quite justifiable, in so far as it recalls the building which formerly stood at the junction of the Epsom and London Roads. Latterly this building was an almshouse for cripples and other poor persons, but originally it was the hostel of the Crutched or Red-cross Friars, and was dedicated to St. Thomas. Holy Trinity Rectory, formerly the Poyle Manor House, now stands on the spot once thus occupied. It may, too, be of interest to record the fact that at the "White House" opposite, now White Hall (Mr. C. J. Sells), William Cobbett was at one time employed as a gardener.

A FLOOD ON THE WEY.
(From a photograph by Mr. T. M. Brownrigg.)

CHAPTER II.

HE Castle Keep, still sternly overlooking the town and its people, is Guildford's most important relic of the past. It recalls, even to-day, the distant years when Guildford was a favourite royal resort, and the close connection formerly existing through many successive generations between the borough and the monarchs of the realm.

But the truth is, nevertheless, that there are few eventful episodes allied with our national history to point to in the Castle's annals. As Mr. Clark[*] has well said, " though of great age, neither the town nor the Castle has played any great part in English history. The town was never walled ; the Castle never stood a siege. No considerable battle was ever witnessed from its towers ; no Parliament or Great Council was ever held within its hall. Though always a Royal Manor, and long maintained as a royal residence, it was used also as a prison, and is but rarely mentioned either in the records or by the chroniclers. The Castle was not garrisoned in the great Civil War, and so escaped being dismantled by either King or Parliament. Its state of decay is due to the effects of time, powerfully aided by the local greed for building materials."

But where fact has failed, conjecture has boldly stepped in, and fancy has sometimes been allowed to have very free play in the pictures which have been drawn of Guildford's past. We have been asked to look upon the Keep as the last vestige of a structure which was one of the palaces of the earliest Saxon kings. One learned antiquary convinced himself that 'it was the dwelling-place of Alfred the Great, and that here the King "measured his well-employed time by his then novel invention of the candle, with divisions notched upon it to tell the

* " Mediæval Military Architecture "

hours.'   With more warrant, but still, perhaps, without convincing proof, the
town has been associated with the terrible massacre of the Norman followers of
Prince Alfred by Earl Godwin in 1036.

These are all debatable points.   We may with more confidence agree with
Mr. Clark that the early history of Guildford, "like its name, savours of the arts
of peace."   True, we to-day know nothing of the first Guild or mercantile community which established itself within our boundaries on the ford of the Wey.
But it has been thought that this earliest Saxon municipality settled on the west
bank of the river, and the theory is supported, to some extent at least, by the
fact that such names as Bury (Burgh) Fields and Bury Street still linger.   The
suggestion has also been thrown out that this choice of the west bank may have
been due to the want of space for private dwellings, consequent upon the erection
of a fortress on the east bank, on the site afterwards occupied by the Castle.
Mr. Clark, however, holds that the reverse was probably the fact.   " A fortress,"
he says, " whether Saxon or Norman, would, as a rule, attract inhabitants to place
themselves under its protection, and however spacious may have been the area
enclosed, there must always have been ample room between the walls and the
river to the north, where the present town is located.   If ever the town
stood upon the west bank, the balance of probability is in favour of its having
been transferred across the stream as soon as the earliest stronghold was
established there."

In any case, we know from authentic records that the town and manor of
Guildford were among the demesnes of Alfred and Edward the Confessor.   We
know, too, that in the days of Ethelred II, Guildford was the seat of a royal
mint, for some coins struck in the town still exist with the name of St. Dunstan
upon them.   Nor must we forget that Malory in the " Morte d'Arthur ' tells
" how King Arthur lodged in a town called Astolat, which is now in English
called Guildford."

The manor passed into the hands of the Conqueror, and from the
Domesday Survey we learn that on the "land of the King" there were
75 houses, occupied by 175 freed men or tenants.   The Conqueror granted
a portion of the Crown lands on the east bank to the Testards, who held it by a
somewhat singular tenure for several generations, and are stated to have built
the churches of St. Mary and Holy Trinity.   Later on this property passed
to Thomas de la Puille, of whom Pewley Hill—the summit of which is now
the site of fortifications carried out by the War Office, as part of a scheme
for the defence of the Metropolis — still reminds us.   The grant to the
Testards, however, left a considerable domain still in the hands of the Crown,
and, judging from its architectural features, the Castle — including in that

SPRING MORNING ON THE WEY.
(From a photograph by Mr. T. M. Brownrigg.)

term the keep, hall, and domestic buildings, and the enceinte wall, enclosing some five acres in all—must have been constructed by Henry II. very shortly after his accession. In 1154 we know that the same monarch, whose love of the chase was keen, formed a large park on the opposite side of the river and north of the Hog's Back, and the Guildford Park of to-day recalls the earlier associations of the site.

Henry was one of several monarchs who found Guildford an attractive temporary place of residence, comparatively easy of access from London, and offering excellent facilities for sport. He spent Christmas here in 1186. It was here that he is believed to have received the Legates of Pope Urban II. when they came to this country to assist in investing Prince John with the Crown of Ireland. It was here, too, according to tradition, that the Prior and monks of St. Swithun's, at Winchester, besought the King's intervention because their Bishop had reduced the number of courses served to them at table from thirteen to ten, and were rebuked for their gluttony in appropriately strong terms by the King.

John, ever restless, was in Guildford nineteen times in seventeen years. On one occasion he kept Christmas at the Castle with much splendour, and equipped his household, we are told, with new liveries, which, to his great but dissembled disgust, the Archbishop of Canterbury proceeded to surpass in magnificence. In 1215 the King spent a week in Guildford after his defeat at Bouvines, actively employed, it has been surmised, in trying to obtain support from the clergy to resist the Barons. His last visit was paid in April, 1216, and in June of the same year the Castle was occupied by Prince Louis of France, when, having landed in Kent at the invitation of the English Peers, he was in pursuit of John at Winchester.

Pleasanter and happier associations gathered round the Castle during the following reign. For, under Henry III.'s direction, the buildings were both enlarged and decorated, and workmen were constantly busy upon them. Henry was a liberal patron of the arts, and not least of architecture, and he paid much attention to the royal residences, Guildford Castle among the number. The Liberate Rolls, quoted in Parker's " Domestic Architecture," tell us of many repairs to the great hall, of the painting of a pallium at the head of the King's bed, of the finishing of the tablets and frontal of the altar, agreeably to the design of William of Florence, the painter, and of other additions and improvements for the special benefit of the King's " dear daughter Eleanor." Yet the town was to have sad memories for Eleanor, for it was in Guildford that her son, Prince Henry, died (1274) after a lengthy illness.

Of the work thus carried out under Henry's directions we have virtually no trace now. Save for a few fragments, the domestic apartments of the Castle have long since disappeared, and we can get no glimpse of the "King's son's chamber, with proper windows well barred," the "narrow pent-house, competently long for the Queen's wardrobe," or the "Queen's chamber, with its large new window and two marble columns." Curiously enough, the Keep, which does not seem to have shared in the royal care, alone retains to-day its original form. Some small portions of the walls of the outer or lower ward—in which (says Mr. Clark) there was of course a large chapel—are still traceable ; and the picturesque Castle arch in Quarry Street still shows the groves for the portcullis. The inner ward was comprised in a space enclosed by the Keep and the circular wall, about twenty-five feet high, which sprang from the south-east angle of the Keep, and seems to have been carried round the mound until it reached the north-east angle, where in all probability there was a gateway. It was in the centre of this inner ward that the hall and principal buildings were situated.

THE LODGE IN THE CASTLE GROUNDS.
(From a photograph by Mr. A. E. Mow.)

The fact that the oldest and strongest portion of the Castle—the Keep itself was not deemed worthy of restoration by Henry is easily understood. For the keeps of such Norman strongholds were inhabited but rarely, and only during a siege, even by those who built them. Not unnaturally, they were sometimes deserted altogether for more convenient apartments. A use, if a somewhat ignoble one, was, nevertheless, found for the Guildford Keep. During the thirteenth century it was entrusted to the Sheriff of Surrey, that it might be utilized as a prison. William de Coniers was Constable of the Castle in 1226, and Elias de Maunsel in 1255 ; and in 1273 an inquiry by commission was instituted as to encroachments on the Castle precincts. In 1305 the then Keeper of the Castle, Henry de Sey, petitioned either for a gaol delivery or for the transfer of some of his prisoners to a more secure stronghold. His prayer was in vain. He was reminded that his chief duty was to keep his prisoners safely, even if he had to double-iron them ; but he was given permission to enlarge and strengthen the building. In the list of the Constables of the Castle only one name of special note is to be found, that of Sir Simon Burley, who held the office under Richard II. Burley, whose virtues and talents are eulogized by Froissart, had been chosen by Edward III. and the Black

Prince to superintend Richard's education. For a time he ranked high among the courtiers of the day, and after his tenure of office at Guildford he became Constable of Dover Castle and Chamberlain to the King. Ultimately, however, he fell a victim to the hatred and treasonable aims of Gloucester, by whom he was denounced as one of "the traitors, whisperers, flatterers, and unprofitable

THE KEEP BEFORE RESTORATION.
(*From a photograph by Mr. G. J. Jacobs*)

people," impoverishing and dishonouring the realm. Despite the entreaties of Anne, he was beheaded on Tower Hill in May, 1388.

For a century or more at this period Guildford Castle seems to have been used as the common gaol for Surrey and Sussex. In 1488 Sussex obtained permission from Parliament to consign their own prisoners to the gaol at Lewes, as "great murderers, thieves, and misdoers" often made their escape whilst in transit across the wild country then to be traversed to reach the Surrey fortress.

We must turn for a few moments to the history of the rest of the royal

3

demesne. In 1299 the park and manor were assigned to Queen Margaret, but on her death, in 1317, they reverted to the Crown, and twenty or thirty years later we find Edward III. resident here. Hastening on, we may note in passing that Edward IV. appears to have visited the town ; that in 1488 the custody of the manor and park was given to Sir Reginald Bray by Henry VII., presumably in acknowledgment of services rendered to the King before his accession ; that Charles Brandon, Duke of Suffolk, Henry's nephew by marriage, died at the Guildford Palace in 1546 ; and that Edward VI. passed some time here in the summer of 1550, and again in 1552, very shortly before his death. Apparently, however, it was not in the Castle that these royal visitors of later days sojourned. For, as I shall have occasion to show in a subsequent chapter, there is a good reason to believe that Henry VIII. followed up the suppression of the Friary at Guildford by repairing and adapting to his own use the buildings formerly belonging to the Dominicans, and standing in close proximity to the royal park.

CASTLE ARCH, QUARRY STREET.
(From a photograph by Mr. G. J. Jacobs.)

After various grants by succeeding monarchs, the manor and park, with specific mention of the Friary, were in 1631 sold by Charles I. to the Earl of Annandale in fee simple. Power was given to dispark the lands, which early in the last century passed into the hands of the Onslow family.

A different fate befell the royal demesne on the east bank of the river, which, after the grant to the Testards, was still Crown property, and on which the Castle itself stood. This land, with the Castle, was granted in 1612 by royal patent to Francis Carter, of the Priory, Guildford. It was held by his descendants till 1813, when it was sold, with houses and buildings in Quarry Street, to Charles, Duke of Norfolk. The Duke's son disposed of it to the late Lord Grantley. The site of the Castle, including the fosse and vallum, were inclosed as part of the grounds of Castle House, for a long time in the occupation of Mr. Elkins, and used during the Assizes as the judge's lodgings. Later on the property was the home of the Castle School, under Dr. Fernandez and Mr. W. Lydgate.

THE KEEP.

At length, however, steps were taken to secure permanently for the town this relic of the past. In 1885 the Grantley property was offered for sale. The Guildford Corporation wisely took advantage of the opportunity, and bought the site of the Castle for £2,200, and, later on, the old Bowling Green adjacent to the Keep. A property was thus acquired which has been admirably turned to account in providing the town with public pleasure-grounds of much interest and beauty. The grounds were laid out, and the ruins judiciously restored, under the direction of Mr. Henry Peak, then borough surveyor, and they were dedicated to the public use by the Mayor (Mr. W. Swayne) on Coronation Day, 1888. The total cost was £6,990, towards which Lord Ashcombe, for many years one of the members of Parliament for the Western Division of the county, generously contributed £1,000.

The Keep stands on the summit of a mound, much, if not all, of which is certainly artificial, and was thrown up by Saxon hands some 200 years before the Norman masons began their work. The walls rise to the height of seventy feet, and vary from eight feet to ten feet in thickness. Within, the Keep is divided into three stories, but the roof and the floorings have long ceased to exist. A theory was at one time held that beneath the ground-floor, as we know it now, there was once a lower floor of dungeons. But the investigations of Mr. H. Peak and Mr. E. L. Lunn during the restoration quite disposed of this conjecture, and refuted also the suggestion that an entrance to these dungeons existed on the south side. As regards the ground-floor, indeed, it should be borne in mind that the present rough archway is comparatively modern, and that the old way of access was from the floor above by a trap-door. Lighted only by two loop-holes four inches wide, the place, without imagining a deeper depth still, was gloomy enough, as Mr. Lunn writes, for consigning any felon to

> "Fetters and the damp vault's dayless gloom,
> Dim with dull imprisoned rays."

The floor above, containing the great hall, was entered by a portal on the west side about fifteen or sixteen feet from the ground. The fact that the exterior arch of this portal is pointed, while the interior arch is semicircular, strikingly indicates the transitional Norman date of the building. Holes on either side of the door served for the insertion of the great beams of strong timber used for the better securing of the entrance. It is lighted by three windows, and remains of the hearth and chimney can be detected on the north side. In the thickness of the wall at the north-west angle is a circular well staircase chamber. Three chambers in the walls also open out from this state room.   One was a small bed-chamber or ante-room ; another was no doubt the oratory or chapel, used also, possibly, as a prison cell when the basement offered insufficient accommodation.   This apartment, the Chapel of St. Christopher, as it has been called, is of particular interest.   At the east end are the remains of two broad steps, which probably indicate the site of the altar.   On the south and a portion of the west sides are the remains of a sculptured Norman arcade, and in the chalk ashlaring of the walls some roughly-executed figures have been carved   Concerning these figures, conjecture has naturally been very busy.   They have been attributed by some writers to soldiers who may have been lodged in the apartment as a guard-room ; by others, to prisoners detained within these walls.   In either case, it seems reasonable to infer that they were not all the work of one hand.   Amongst the subjects depicted are the representation of the crucifixion, with a soldier piercing the Saviour's side, and the Virgin fainting, an Agnus Dei, a man scourging a female figure, St. Christopher bearing the Infant Jesus in his arms, a king and queen kneeling, and a square pilaster with sculptured ornaments on the capital, similar to several in the undercroft at Canterbury.   It is unfortunate that many acts of vandalism, committed before the ruins were in the possession of the Corporation, have robbed this chamber of much of the unique interest which would otherwise have attached to it.

On the floor above there was on each side a recess or passage corresponding to those on the state apartment beneath.   In addition, a passage in the south wall some five feet long leads to an over-hanging machicolation pierced with two large openings, which project beyond the exterior surface of the wall. The original timber roof was surrounded by a parapet, and it is thought that a turret existed at either corner.   In 1888 an iron-work erection was put up at the top of the Keep, and if it certainly does not add to the picturesqueness of the ruin, it at least secures the safety of those who mount thither to enjoy a wide and lovely landscape.

A few words ought to be added here with respect to the caverns in the chalk ridge on which the Castle stands.   They consist in all of some eight chambers, the largest 105 feet long, and varying from 15 feet to 28 feet in width, and from 5 feet to 7 feet in height from floor to floor.   They remained for years unexplored, until attention was called to them during the ordnance survey of 1868, and, naturally enough, they have provoked almost as much speculation as the Keep itself.   At one time they were thought to have communicated with the Castle buildings.   But this theory was completely disproved twenty years ago by General James, who showed that the caves did not underlie the site of the Castle, that their northern extremity is 100 yards from the Keep and 176 feet below it, and that 65 feet of solid chalk intervene between the surface of the ground and the roof of the cave nearest the Castle. Nor is there better warrant for the popular tradition once current that the caverns were torture-chambers—unless, indeed, we find it in the name Rack Close. It seems much more reasonable to suppose, as General James argues, that the caverns were originally chalk quarries. We need not go a step farther with the General, and endorse his conjecture that possibly they date from Roman or pre-Roman times ; but we may give due weight to his reminder that no chalk of the same kind is now quarried in the neighbourhood, though much of a similar description is to be seen embedded in the lower walls of the Castle Keep and St. Mary's Church, as well as in Compton and Alfold Churches.

One assumption, however, we may perhaps fairly make. Possibly it was in these caverns that Henry III. kept the large stock of French wines, which the Sheriff was ordered to dispose of in the town, and to permit no others to be sold in his bailiwick meanwhile. Another legend may, too, be legitimately linked with these caves. It is related that, soon after the accession of William and Mary, a report prevailed that the Irish had landed in England, and were massacring all whom they met, without regard to age or sex. The report, we are told, "struck such terror into the inhabitants that great numbers of men, women, and children hid themselves in these subterraneous caverns."

Panic-stricken Guildfordians could surely not wish or hope for a safer hiding-place.

A FRAGMENT OF THE CASTLE RUINS.
(From a photograph by Mr. G. J. Jacobs.)

CHAPTER III.

HE municipal life of Guildford, symbolized by the Town Hall, which with its quaint and picturesque front and its projecting clock-dial is such a conspicuous feature of the High Street. spans some six centuries or more. In these pages I can make no attempt to note much that the careful local historian can tell us of the various vicissitudes which in this long series of years befell the borough in respect of its municipal rights and responsibilities. I can but chronicle a few of the salient incidents and characteristics of the past.

In this past the Guild Merchant figures largely. Indeed, the town's very name, and the fact that the Town Hall is also the Guildhall, suggest the close relationship subsisting between this early organization for the defence and promotion of local trade and the corporate life of the community. What, then, was this Guild Merchant, which grew up side by side with the burgh-mote, and ultimately, after the lapse of many years, absorbed the latter's duties and rights? At first the Guild Merchant was mainly a private society unconnected with town government. Its sole aim was the maintenance of trade and the protection of the interests of its members, the tradesmen of the borough. In Guildford, as elsewhere, however, it became later on a recognised part of the town constitution. For, as from the outset it was composed of the most influential burgesses, it was only natural that to it should gradually be assigned an important part of the civic administration. By the end of the thirteenth century this process was complete, and a further period of transition was begun which, a hundred years later still, left the Guild without an individuality of its own. Its identity was merged in that of the general municipal organism, its presiding officer was now the head of the town; "borough and guild, burgesses and guildsmen, were now identical."* Yet the old dual idea, as

* "The Guild Merchant," by Dr. Gross.

Dr. Gross aptly puts it, did not completely disappear, the Guild being often regarded as a particular phase or function of the town, viz., the municipality as a trade monopoly. In a few boroughs the select governing body of the town, the narrow civic corporation, in distinction from the burgesses or freemen at large, succeeded to the name and traditions of the Guild Merchant. We must note, too, that, vague and meaningless as the term had become, it still tenaciously clung to some town muniments. Thus it is found sometimes in the eighteenth century; by the beginning of the nineteenth it was very rare, though still figuring, as we shall presently see, in the Guildford records.

One further fact should be borne in mind : that is, the extent to which the affiliation of boroughs took place in the thirteenth and fourteenth centuries. When a prosperous village or newly - founded town wished to procure the franchise of a free borough, or when a borough sought an extension of its liberties, it looked for a model among its more privileged and prosperous neighbours. Its townspeople would then negotiate with their lord for the grant of some or all of the privileges which this more favoured community enjoyed.

If in the light of these broad facts we turn to the history of our own municipality, we learn something from the statement quoted in Root's " Kingston Charities." that Henry III. in 1256 "granted the men of Kingston-upon-Thames the Guild Merchant just as the men of Guildford had it." The significance of this circumstance is indeed twofold. It chronicles the affiliation of Kingston-on-Thames to Guildford, and throws light upon the first charter of incorporation, dated 1257, of which we in Guildford have any trace. This charter confirmed the approved men of the borough in the enjoyment of various rights and privileges which had been conferred before. But of the exact date of the earlier charter or charters, the existence of which the Kingston records so plainly point to, we have, and apparently can have now, no knowledge. A few months later, in 1257, another charter ordered the removal of the County Court or Assize from Leatherhead to Guildford, and as the provision of a shire hall was in this way rendered necessary, we may perhaps assume that the foundations of the first counterpart of our present Town Hall were laid at this period.

Two subsequent charters (Edward III.), 1341 and 1346, call for notice only in so far as the former granted a five days' fair, and the latter altered the date of the fixture from Trinity Eve to Whitsun Monday.

The charter granted in 1366 by the same King is, however, more noteworthy. It gave the burgesses (1) the fee farm of the town at an annual rent of £10, the King reserving the Castle, Gaol, and Park ; and (2) the privileges of a Merchant Guild as at Winchester. It empowered the steward (*i.e.*, Mayor)

4

and bailiff to act as justices of the peace. Thus, just as Kingston had eighty years before been affiliated to Guildford, so now Guildford was affiliated to Winchester, one of the great mother towns of the country.

Passing by the subsequent confirmation of these rights, we come to the important charter granted by Henry VII. in 1489. This document secured to the burgesses many privileges. It exempted them from every kind of toll by land or water throughout England. It granted them a Court every three weeks before the Mayor and two burgesses, to which large powers were assigned. It authorized a Court of Piepowder for the regulation of fairs, and it granted also two annual fairs, one on the eve and day of St. Martin's, and the other on the eve and day of St. George. But, further, the charter is significant because it established the familiar term of Mayor in local usage. Hitherto the officials of the Guild Merchant at Guildford had been a steward (or seneschal), four farthing-men, a clerk, a marshal, four cup-bearers, and two hall wardens. This charter of Henry VII., however, incorporated the town under the title of the Mayor and Burgesses, and entrusted the administration of the town's affairs to " the Mayor and approved men "—a designation which was to hold good for two or three centuries.

The new governing body, despite its enlarged powers and heightened status, long held fast to the traditions of the Guild Merchant. They " protected " local trade with all possible vigour, and heavily fined " foreigners " before permitting them to sell or buy within the borough. A few examples of this fostering care, as recent as the reign of James I., may be recalled. In 1612 seven shoemakers were fined for selling shoes " not well made, and making mixture of leather in shoes and botes contrary to the statute, taking excessive gaine." Eight " fishers " and nine cooks were similarly punished for selling unwholesome fish and flesh, and for selling flesh in Lent. But neither public morals nor public pastimes were forgotten. A beadle from every parish was ordered " to peruse " and go round to all the ale-houses during the hours of divine service, where " men servants and other poor men often tarried " when they ought to be in church. Attendance at church before market on Saturdays was vigorously enforced, and the sanctity of the Sabbath was stoutly upheld. Under these circumstances, it is hardly surprising that the town authorities found it incumbent to punish and imprison " deriders," that is, those who openly taunted and jested at " anything done, or to be done, by good and lawful men sworne for mayntenance of good rule." But let it be remembered also to the credit of our forefathers that they were not unmindful of the less serious side of life. They sanctioned and encouraged bull and bear baiting, and in a spirit certainly not extinct in the present day, they insisted that every new member of the

EXTERIOR OF THE TOWN HALL.

Corporation should provide his brethren on his election with "breakfast and a bull-running." When we reach the days of Elizabeth the bull-running no longer appears on the municipal programme, but the feasting was still observed, and no doubt enjoyed.

From the later chapters of our municipal history I can quote only a few leading incidents. When, in the seventeenth century, the country was rent with civil strife, Guildford's sympathies were distinctly with the King. In 1648 the town was the scene of a meeting which formally petitioned both Houses of Parliament that Charles might be restored to his due honours, and "come to

INTERIOR OF THE HALL.

his Parliament for a personal treaty." The Restoration, in 1660, was heartily welcomed, and when, in September of that year, Charles II. honoured the town with a special visit, the Corporation agreed to present his Majesty with a service of plate, and entertain him at a suitable banquet. To meet the outlay involved, however, the sum of £100 had to be borrowed.

But the burgesses very speedily found grave cause for repenting this extravagant rejoicing. The Corporation Act of 1661 made a serious inroad on their rights and liberties. In common with every other Corporation in the country, they suffered still more severely under James II. The town charter had to be surrendered to the King in compliance with his determined efforts to shut out all but ultra-loyalists from the local-governing bodies. Guildford, in return, received a charter, dated April 15, 1686, which registered this surrender of the old charter, nominated new officers under the names of Mayor, High Steward, Recorder, Aldermen, Common Council, and Bailiffs, and acknowledged the power of the King at his mere will to remove any of these officials. As a very doubtful solatium, the Mayor and Aldermen were accorded the permission. of which they still avail themselves, to wear scarlet gowns.

James did not scruple to use these powers, and in the following year an ever-memorable episode was witnessed in the town's history. Thomas Smith, the then Mayor, two Aldermen, and three Councillors were removed from the Corporation by the King's orders, and nominees of the Crown were appointed in their place. This process was repeated in April, 1688, when the Recorder, the Town Clerk, two Aldermen, and three more Councillors were similarly deposed. The arbitrary action of James, of which this was but one specimen. in the long run defeated its own ends. The King had to retrace his steps, and practically acknowledge himself vanquished by the people whom he had attempted to overawe. A royal proclamation, dated October of the same year, restored to all Corporations their original charters, and Guildford was once more in full possession of its ancient rights. The most notable proof of this triumph is, perhaps, to be found in the fact that Thomas Smith, the ejected Mayor of 1687, was reinstated in office.

From these closing years of the seventeenth century till the great Municipal Reform of 1835, the government of the town continued unchanged on the lines laid down in the Jacobean charter. There were eight magistrates or aldermen. and an undefined number, rarely exceeding twenty or twenty-five, of bailiffs or councillors. The Mayor was chosen from the magistrates on the Monday after Michaelmas Day ; the magistrates, when a vacancy occurred, were selected for life from the bailiffs ; and a new bailiff was chosen each year simultaneously with the election of a mayor. The High Steward and the Recorder were also among the Corporation officials. The last meeting of the Guild Merchant was held on October 14, 1806.

Much feasting was still the order of the day. The Mayor was expected to give a public supper to a large company on the evening of his inauguration, a dinner to the High Steward and Council at Christmas, and a "public dinner" in the autumn. A newly-elected bailiff—"the bailiff for the year"—was expected to feast the Corporation from time to time during his term of office. Even so, the round of municipal festivities was not entirely exhausted.

Hospitality on a similarly lavish scale was also part of the recognised duties of the Town Clerk and the High Steward.

Thus matters went on till 1835, when Guildford came within the scope of the changes effected by the Municipal Corporations Act. By this Statute the Corporation was reduced to the modest proportions it still retains, viz., four Aldermen and twelve Councillors. A further extension of the borough boundaries, which must bring with it an enlargement of the Council and the division of the town into wards, is certainly among the possibilities of the near future.

From this brief glance at the municipal history of the borough we may

INTERIOR OF THE COUNCIL CHAMBER.

turn to the Town Hall itself. A portion of the building, it has been assumed, dates back to Elizabeth. The old market-house or Guild " stood across the street." When this obstruction to the traffic was pulled down, the present building was erected (1683) by public subscription, and it is rightly prized to-day as one of the most picturesque Guildhalls in the South of England. The projecting clock dial—the clock was the gift of Mr. J. Aylward in return for his freedom—the carved woodwork which covers the brick front, the balcony supported by four grotesque figures as brackets, the open turret, containing a bell which is alleged to have been brought early last century from St. Martha's Chapel, are the external features which combine to give the building a character and a charm of its own. In the Hall on the ground-floor several of the town pictures claim notice. The two full-length portraits of Charles II. and James II. (when Duke of York) are by Lely. The town records do not tell us how these came into the possession of the Corporation; but Mr. Whitburn has surmised that they were painted for John, Duke of Lauderdale, in 1674, and presented by him to the Borough upon his creation as Earl of Guildford. Similarly, Mr. Whitburn suggests that the portraits of Queen Mary and William III., which he attributes to John Riley, and which are also hung in the Hall, may have been the gift of Francis North, who succeeded to the Barony of Guildford in 1685.

FIREPLACE IN THE COUNCIL CHAMBER.

Greater local interest attaches to two of the portraits in the Council Chamber on the floor above. One represents Vice-Admiral Sir Richard Onslow receiving the Dutch flag after the victory at Camperdown in 1797, and was painted by John Russell, R.A., of whom I shall have more to say hereafter. It was presented to the town by the artist's father, John Russell, during his mayoralty. The portrait of the Right Hon. Arthur Onslow, Speaker of the House of Commons, Mr. Whitburn attributes to Jonathan Richardson, and that of James I. to Paul Van Somer, adding the conjecture that it may have been given to the town by Archbishop Abbot.

The most curious feature of the Council Chamber is, however, the massive chimney-piece brought from Stoughton Manor House. The figures in the four compartments are devised to illustrate different human temperaments. Sanguineus shows us the lover vowing devotion to his mistress ; Cholericus

THE TOWN PLATE, ETC.

depicts the soldier surrounded by martial devices ; Phlegmaticus is typified by a stolid individual in a boat taking a landing of fish ; and Melancholicus is a solitary figure deep in thought.

A few words as to the Town Plate, some items of which exceptionally well deserve notice. The Mayor's staff of ebony, with a silver top, was a gift from Elizabeth. It bears the motto, "Fayre God, doe Justice. Love thy Brother." The handsome silver basin and ewer, which date from the same

5

reign, were presented by Bishop Parkhurst to the Corporation of his native town. The larger of the two maces was presented, in 1663, by the Right Honourable Henry Howard, then High Steward, and afterwards Duke of Norfolk. The smaller mace dates back still further. The donor is unknown ; but Mr. Hope, the secretary of the Society of Antiquaries, attributes its workmanship to the latter part of the fifteenth century, and considers it the third oldest in the kingdom. The Mayor's chain was given by Mr. Arthur Onslow.

From the balcony of the Town Hall has been announced the news of the issue of many a stubbornly-fought political contest. In the earliest days of our Parliamentary history Guildford had the privilege of sending two burgesses to the Legislature, and the Austen extracts from the Black Book inform us that in Edward III.'s time these representatives were remunerated at the rate of 1s. per day. During the Commonwealth the borough lost one of its members, but the dual representation was restored after Cromwell's death. Maurice Abbot, the Mores, and Carew Raleigh (only son of Sir Walter, and then living at West Horsley Place), were among the representatives of the borough, and in 1679 Algernon Sydney unsuccessfully sued the suffrages of the electors. In subsequent years, the Onslows and Mr. Morgan Randyll practically controlled the nominal choice of the "free and independent burgesses," and throughout the four Georges the Onslows figure almost without break in the list, though honours were sometimes divided with a member of Lord Grantley's family. At the last contest (1831) before the Great Reform Bill, the polling was: Mangles 100, Norton 83, Summer 73, Wall 55. These figures are, of course, in themselves suggestive enough of the character of the constituency, and no great effort of the imagination is needed to conceive some elements of the fight under the "good old" system of free and open voting, and its customary accompaniments.

The Reform Act still left the borough a couple of members, and this right was enjoyed until 1868, when one member was lost. The redistribution of seats in 1885 brought a still further change by the merging of the borough in the newly-formed Guildford or South-Western Parliamentary Division of Surrey.

CHAPTER IV

T is only fitting that the two Onslow portraits, to which reference has just been made, should find a permanent home in the Town Hall, for no name figures in the town's history more frequently or more conspicuously than that of Onslow. Turn where or when one will in the local records for the past three or four centuries, some instance is sure to be discovered of the close connection which has long subsisted between the family and the borough. Year by year, after the accession of the House of Hanover, the Onslows shared, when they did not monopolize, the Parliamentary representation of Guildford. An Onslow was High Steward in the seventeenth century—one of his descendants holds the same position to-day. Several members of the family have been the Borough Recorder. And from time to time in the town's affairs the Onslows have joined hands with their neighbours when local effort or public generosity was called for.

Of the goodwill thus manifested to the borough in the past much tangible evidence now remains. The "faire chaine of gold double-linked, with a medal of massey gold, whereon His Majestie's armes are curiously engraven," still worn by the Mayors of Guildford, was the gift of Arthur Onslow, High Steward in 1673. The handsome two-volume illustrated Bible (Vinegar edition), still to be seen at Holy Trinity Church, was presented by another and still more distinguished Arthur Onslow in 1738. The set of Prayer-books still used by the Corporation on the occasion of State visits to the Church, was the gift of George Onslow in 1763, whilst member for the borough. Nearly a hundred years before, Sir Richard Onslow had been a munificent supporter of the project for the union of the parishes of Holy Trinity and St. Mary. George, first Earl of Onslow, contributed the greater portion of the cost of the clock erected in Holy Trinity tower in 1790; and one of the most interesting monuments in the Church is that which represents the great Speaker Onslow reclining on an altar-tomb in, curiously enough, a " Roman habit."

Although some reference in these pages to the history of the family is, therefore, clearly called for, a brief glance at its records is all that can be attempted. Originally settled in Shropshire—the surname, we are told, was assumed from the lordship of Ondeslow, situated within the liberty of Shrewsbury—the marriage of Richard Onslow in the sixteenth century to Catherine, heir and daughter of Richard Harding, of Knoll, or Knowle, in Cranley (now Cranleigh), was the first link in the chain of association with the county of Surrey and the town of Guildford. Moreover, this Richard Onslow was the first of his name to make his mark in the public life of the country. A barrister by profession, he seems to have risen rapidly to the front rank. He became successively Recorder of the City of London, Attorney-General of the Duchy of Lancaster, Solicitor-General, and, finally, Speaker of the House of Commons. He does not appear to have won his way upward by undue submission to Court influence, for, before his elevation to the chair, he took part in the sturdy efforts of the Commons throughout Elizabeth's reign to maintain the liberty of the subject, and to define and circumscribe the prerogatives of the monarch. Thus Hallam mentions that Onslow, in 1566, and whilst Solicitor-General, clearly laid down the principle in addressing the Queen, that "although there be for the Prince provided many princely prerogatives and royalties, yet it is not such as the Prince can take money or other things to do as he will at his own pleasure without order, but quietly to suffer his subjects to enjoy their own without wrongful oppression." Good sound doctrine, assuredly.

His grandson, Richard, succeeded to the estate in 1616, and eight years afterwards obtained the honour of knighthood from James I. Locally the most noteworthy incident in his life was the purchase of Clandon Lodge from Sir Richard Weston, of Sutton. One or two episodes in his public career, however, call for passing notice. Sir Richard served in three Parliaments for the county of Surrey, and was a somewhat prominent member of the Parliamentary party. But as one of the sequestrators of the estates of the Surrey Royalists (1643), he did not escape a charge of disaffection to the popular cause. This was levelled against him by George Wither (the poet), in a pamphlet entitled " Justiciarius Justificatus." The matter was brought to the notice of the House of Commons, and the accusation having been denounced as false, scandalous, and injurious, Wither was fined £500, and his book was ordered to be burned at Guildford and Kingston markets.

How Sir Richard viewed the subsequent course of affairs under Cromwell's more or less despotic rule we cannot tell, but he was conspicuous among those

who, in 1657, urged the Protector to assume the Crown and the royal title. He was, in fact, a member of the select committee appointed by the Commons to place these views before Cromwell, and to endeavour to remove the doubts and scruples which led the Protector to decline the proffered honour. Perhaps we may assume that Sir Richard Onslow shared the opinions of those who urged this course upon Cromwell, in the belief that it would both remove doubts as to the succession, and place a well-defined limit upon the prerogatives of a ruler whose despotic powers might otherwise be controlled only by his ability to retain the loyal support of his army. In any case, Sir Richard a few years later welcomed and helped to facilitate the Restoration, and was one of the members for Guildford in the Parliament which recalled Charles II. He died in 1664, and was buried at Cranleigh.

The second Speaker Onslow was Sir Richard's grandson Richard. He sat as one of the representatives of Surrey in the Convention Parliament, which was assembled in consequence of the flight of James II. In 1708 he was chosen Speaker, and six years afterwards, on the accession of George I., he became one of the Lords of the Treasury and Chancellor of the Exchequer : two years later still he was created Baron Onslow.

It is to the Baron's nephew Arthur, son of Foot Onslow, and great-grandson of the Sir Richard prominent in the Commonwealth times, that the family chiefly and specially owes its high position and lasting fame in our Parliamentary history. Arthur Onslow held office as Speaker from 1727 till 1761 : throughout, in fact, the whole reign of George II. Coxe, in a somewhat laboured sentence, tells us that Onslow was elected to the post "with an unanimity which could only be inspired by an opinion of his integrity and abilities, an opinion which his subsequent conduct fully justified by an able and impartial discharge of his duty." The test to which both the ability and the integrity of the Speaker were put was indeed severe. For thirty-three years Onslow lived in the heart and centre of English political life. He was an eye-witness of the great constitutional struggle of the eighteenth century between Crown and Parliament. He saw Walpole in the plenitude of his power, and saw him at length overcome by the foes he had so obstinately fought. He saw the ruin and fall of the Pelham Ministry. He was still in the Speaker's chair when the miserable incapacity of the Duke of Newcastle, Byng's shame, and the accumulated disasters of 1757 brought about a national despondency without parallel in our history. But he lived long enough also to witness the magnificent success of Pitt's efforts to shake off this fear and sloth, and to hear of Clive's marvellous triumphs in the far East, and of Wolfe's death in the hour of victory on the Heights of Abraham. These eventful times, moreover, were also times to try severely the integrity of any politician.   Corruption was universal and almost all-powerful.   Walpole was "always ready to pay the price of any man worth having "; the Duke of Newcastle " knew better than any living man the price of every member."

It is no small praise, then, to say of Speaker Onslow that the justice of

THE ONSLOW MONUMENT IN HOLY TRINITY CHURCH.

Coxe's eulogium on his uprightness is acknowledged on all hands.   Lord Stanhope wrote that " Onslow filled the chair with higher merit probably than anyone either before or after him ; with unequalled impartiality, dignity, and courtesy."   Still more emphatic was the testimony of the House of Commons itself. By a unanimous vote of March 18, 1761, the House formally thanked its Speaker " for his constant and unwearied attendance in the chair during the course of about thirty-three years, in five successive Parliaments; for the unshaken integrity and steady impartiality of his conduct there; for the indefatigable pains he has with uncommon abilities constantly taken to promote the real interest of his King and country, to maintain the honour and dignity of Parliament, and to preserve inviolable the rights and privileges of the Commons

THE HILLIER ALMSHOUSES, FARNHAM ROAD.

of Great Britain." It was at the special request of the House that a pension of £3,000 a year was granted to the retiring Speaker.

All, indeed, that we know of Arthur Onslow's mind and character tends to show that this frank and generous recognition of long and faithful service was justly bestowed. Coxe quotes, and Mr. John Morley in his monograph on Walpole endorses, Onslow's judgment on several of the chief political questions of the time, *e.g.*, his perception of the importance of the passing of the Septennial Bill, as marking the emancipation of the Commons from its former dependence on the Crown and the House of Lords; his abhorrence of persecuting "any sort of men because of their religious opinions "; and his opposition to the partial reversal of the attainder of Bolingbroke. Upon one

6

aspect of his character light is thrown by the prayer quoted by Brayley from a Prayer-book in the Onslow seat in West Clandon Church, and composed by the Speaker in the year in which he took office. "Suffer me," runs a part of this petition, "O thou Great Judge and Disposer of all things, to be a suppliant to Thee for the forgiveness of my past offences, and for the directions of Thy Spirit in my future goings, that I may do justly, love mercy, and walk humbly before Thee, my God. Permit me also to implore the continuance of Thy goodness to my family, my friends, my country, and to all the rest of mankind, that justice and truth may govern the world, and the adoring Thee be the chief honour of all nations."

Dying in 1768, the ex-Speaker was buried in the family vault at Merrow. The inscription on his monument in Holy Trinity Church—whose bells forty years before had joyfully proclaimed his elevation to the highest position a Commoner can attain—records the various other offices he held. It adds also that he was "the sixth almost in succession of his name and family who had been burgesses in Parliament for this Borough; the sixth in like manner who had been Knight of the Shire for the County; and the third who had been Speaker of the House of Commons." To this remarkable record both the Onslows and the burgesses of Guildford may surely point with justifiable pride.

Admiral Sir Richard Onslow, whose portrait in oils by John Russell also hangs in the Town Hall, won fame in a different sphere. Born in 1741, he entered the navy, and as the century drew to a close, he shared in one of the series of great naval and military triumphs which help to form a memorable chapter in the history of the younger Pitt. Admiral Onslow was second in command when the English, under Admiral Duncan, met and after obstinate combat almost annihilated the Dutch fleet off Camperdown. Russell, in the painting just named, depicts him in the act of receiving the Dutch colours. His reward from his Sovereign was the well-earned honour of a baronetcy.

It seems only fitting to add that the traditions of the family in respect of active participation in the public service have been consistently upheld by the present Earl as a member of the Salisbury Administration from 1886 to 1888, and as Governor of New Zealand from 1889 to 1892.

Clandon Park, as we have seen, passed into the hands of Sir Richard Onslow in the middle of the seventeenth century, and thither the family removed from Cranleigh after the Revolution of 1688. The present mansion was erected in or about 1730 for the second Baron Onslow from the designs of a Venetian architect, Giacomo Leoni. It is a somewhat strange mixture of styles, for the eastern front is English, the western French, and the south Italian in character. But the result is by no means ineffective, and internally the apartments are large

THE HALL, CLAYDON HOUSE.

and stately. The great hall, which is some forty feet square, is specially noticeable for the two marble chimney-pieces sculptured by Rysbrack. One represents a sacrifice to Bacchus, the other a sacrifice to Diana. The park was considerably enlarged by George, first Earl of Onslow, and was laid out under the direction of the landscape gardener who gained notoriety as " Capability Brown."

The picturesque almshouses in Farnham Road are another link between the Onslows and Guildford. Originally founded in Curtain Road, Shoreditch, in 1800 by Elizabeth Hillier, they were considerably enlarged twelve years later by Nathaniel Hillier, brother of the foundress. In 1879, when removal from London and a further enlargement were decided upon, the prettily-designed houses now occupied by the inmates were built on land abutting on the Farnham Road, which was given by the present Earl of Onslow, the great-great-nephew of the original founder.

CHAPTER V.

HE "coming of the Friars" meant much to mediæval England. It was a religious revival for which the time was as ripe here as on the Continent. Sloth and corruption had crept over and enfeebled the Church. Bishops were worldly and self-seeking ; canons and monks purchased from Rome exemptions to shield the scandal of their lives ; priests were ignorant or idle. Naturally enough, under these circumstances, the begging friars, who trusted to the alms of the poor for their sustenance, who preached the Gospel with unflagging fervour in language familiar and intelligible to peasant and artisan, and who zealously strove to do the work left undone by canon, monk, and priest, gained a hearty welcome, and ultimately found for themselves a permanent home in many a country town.

Guildford in the thirteenth century was no exception to this rule. We know little of the local life of the Carmelites or White Friars, to whose settlement in the High Street I have already referred. Nor can we now say much of the doings of the Crutched or Red-cross Friars in their hostel at the junction of the Epsom and London Roads. But of the Dominicans or Black Friars some records, however slight, still exist. In Friary Street and Friary parish, long without a church, but now incorporated in the district assigned to St. Saviour's, we have memorials of their presence here which even to-day serve to carry back our thoughts to the time when a small religious house stood on the banks of the Wey, and was one of the chief centres of spiritual activity in the old town.

The establishment of this body in Guildford has been generally attributed to Eleanor of Provence, wife of Henry III. It has been further suggested that Eleanor and her daughter-in-law, Eleanor of Castile, wife of Edward I., promoted this settlement in Guildford after the death of Prince Henry (1274) in the town, as " a home wherein perpetual memory of their lost one could be cherished." But the latter theory scarcely seems tenable, for we hear of the existence of " a convent " at Guildford in 1258. Above all, it is clear from a very valuable article on the history of the Friary by Mr. G. C. Williamson, to which I am much indebted, that nearly eight months before Prince Henry's death, Edward I. gave the friars permission to enlarge their ground by taking in a road leading from the town to the King's Park.

However this may be, we know that the home of the Black Friars was situated on the east bank of the Wey, near the spot now occupied by the old Militia Depot and square.* A drawbridge connected with the King's Park across the river, and there seems some warrant for the suggestion, for which I have to thank Dr. H. Taylor, that the meadows known as the Walnut Tree Close were at one time part of their domain. Monastic houses often had walnut plantations, and in a ground plan of the Great Abbey at Bury St. Edmund's a large plot is assigned to the walnut-tree close.

Alas! that we can learn nothing of the early work of the Friars in our midst. "What would we not give," asks Dr. Jessopp very truly, "to know the history, say, during only twenty years of the Preaching Friars in England?" In the dearth of authentic local record we can only piece together, from gleanings elsewhere, a faint picture of their activities and mode of life in Guildford. We can fancy the small band of first arrivals, pledged to poverty, content at the outset with the humblest abode on the banks of the Wey

THE FRIARY MANSION.
(Originally drawn for Russell's " History of Guildford.)

—perhaps even glad to shelter themselves, like the first Franciscans in London, in "cells constructed like sheep cotes, mere wattels with mouldy hay or straw between them." Perhaps, too, as at Canterbury, they "had a very hard time of it. Sometimes a kind soul would bring them actually a dish of meat, sometimes even a bottle of wine ; but as a rule, their fare was bread, made up into twists, we hear, when it was specially excellent—wheat bread, wholesome and palatable, but, alas! sometimes barley bread, washed down with beer too sour to drink undiluted with water." However housed or fed, we can readily

---

* With excellent judgment and foresight, the Friars provided themselves with a supply of pure water from a well on what was the Foxenden Field, close to the London Road Station. The early wooden pipes, and the later leaden ones, with which the supply was conveyed to the Friary, have been occasionally discovered in the course of agricultural and other work.

believe that they spared no effort in discharging the mission that had brought them hither. We can picture them preaching to the townspeople with something of the eloquence which had won Archbishop Langton's favour for the first Dominicans who landed on our shores. We can believe that in Guildford, as in other towns, they sought out the sick and suffering, gladly rendered to the lowest the most menial offices, and sought by self-denial to exemplify, as by homely and fervent sermons to proclaim, the Gospel of Love.

For surely it was thus in Guildford, as elsewhere, that the Dominicans won their way to the heart of peasant and peer alike. So far as the Guildford settlement is concerned, indeed, we know that gifts from Edward, who did so much to help the Black Friars in London, and other benefactors, enabled them in time to build a church and "great house," with a dormitory or upper chamber. Their proximity to the royal park doubtless secured them presents of deer and game, and in Edward's immediate successors they had kindly patrons. Edward III. visited them on several occasions, and the Friars, twenty in number, went in procession to meet and welcome him on his arrival in the town in 1336. Henry VI. and the royal family lodged with the Friars in 1442-43, and left 40s. as largesse for the damage done in entertaining them. Henry VII. granted the Friars firewood from his park, and, among many other benefactors, Sir Reginald Bray, who, as we have seen, was custodian of the royal manor and park, bequeathed £200 for masses for his own soul, and the souls of his wife, father, and mother.

But the Friars were to fall on evil days as the sixteenth century opened. Poverty overtook them. In 1537 we find the order in Guildford humbly suing the King for assistance, and in response they were awarded a small pension. This pension, however, if ever paid, soon ceased, and the little community, shrunk alike in numbers, wealth, and influence, were to be among the victims of Henry's ruthless anti-Church policy. It has been aptly said that in Cromwell's system, in pursuance of this policy, there was no room for either the virtues or the vices of monasticism. But the truth is also that in Henry's time the Friars had lost much of the fervour of devotion and self-sacrificing zeal which had made them a religious force two centuries before. The position they had won had been abused. They had gained in worldly goods ; but they had fallen from their former high estate as men who sought only to bring the sinner to repentance. By degrees they sank to the level of the Church they had originally striven to bring back to a sense of her duty, and became a source, not of strength, but of weakness to the cause of true religion. Thus we are told that the special license which the Guildford Friars received from the Bishop of Winchester to hear confessions and to preach in the diocese

HOAR FROST AT ARLINGTON HOUSE.
(From a photograph by Mr. T. M. Brownrigg.)

was productive of irregularity and disorder. It encroached on the privileges of the parochial clergy, and it was a snare to their people. The former lost control of their flocks; the latter could easily evade their religious obligations. Confession and penance became trivial matters, and the Friars who heard the one and imposed the other were ridiculed and burlesqued by the wits of the day.

When the blow was struck, and all but the great abbeys were called upon to surrender to the King, the Friary at Guildford did not escape. The "visit of desolation" was paid, and the house surrendered to Henry's Commissioners on October 10, 1538; henceforth the Guildford Friary as a religious house ceased to exist.

SUNSET ON THE PEASMARSH.
(From a photograph by Mr. T. M. Brownrigg.)

The original deed of surrender was found, by the Rev. C. Kerry, late of Puttenham, among the Patent Rolls at the Record Office. It bears the signatures of the seven brethren who then formed the community, and with it is an interesting inventory of the contents of the Friary. The latter document makes it clear that the church possessed a choir or chancel, a central tower and nave, a chantry chapel and a vestry, and that the domestic buildings included two kitchens—one large, the other small—each containing its inner house, and separated by a passage, a pantry or bakehouse with ovens, the great room or great house, and a dormitory or upper chamber.

It was long held that Henry, when he had once secured possession of the building, erected a new house on the site of the old home of the Friars, and that this new house was considered the principal house in the royal manor, and was probably the temporary residence of the King in 1546, and of Edward VI. a few years later. Mr. Kerry's researches, however, point to a different conclusion, and give colour to the supposition that the King merely repaired the existing buildings and made them more suitable for his use. Two letters among the Loseley MSS. tend perhaps to confirm this view. On August 27, 1571, Lord Burleigh wrote to Sir William More, and mentioned that after viewing the Friary he made a rude sketch of it with his own hand. On September 27, 1575, Viscount Montague wrote to Sir William More concerning the recent outbreaks of fire at "Gilford Manor House," where "the ghost of a monk or friar" greatly alarmed Mrs. Fuller, who, with her husband, were the sole occupants at the time. These small scraps of evidence, although they clearly point to the continued existence of the old house, do not carry us very far. We are on safer ground in recording that James I., soon after his accession, demised the estate to Sir George More of Loseley. In April, 1606, it was leased by Sir George to Mr. George Austen, and the deed, preserved among the Loseley MSS., covenants for the removal within one year "of all the timber, tile, brick and stone which might be had or taken of the old great kitchen, and all the stone wall of the said great house courtyard westward." George Austen duly carried out this covenant, and documents in the possession of Lieutenant-Colonel Godwin Austen point to the conclusion that some at least of the materials so obtained were used in the erection of Shalford House. Apparently, then, the final demolition of the old Friary took place not later than 1608. If the tradition is well founded that the fine stained glass in the chapel of Holy Trinity Hospital came from the Friary, it would no doubt be at this time that Abbot secured it. But though one contemporary authority states emphatically that this was the case, the point is much in dispute. The windows, it has been urged, were plainly altered expressly for the chapel of the hospital, and perhaps the more reasonable theory is that some of the lights may have originally belonged to the Friary, and were utilized by the Archbishop by

incorporating them with other glass for the windows which form one of the chief beauties of the hospital chapel.

It was not till Lord Annandale, in 1630, obtained an absolute grant in fee simple of the royal lands, including the Friary, that any fresh erection was begun on the old site. This mansion, of which the woodcut on page 35 conveys some idea, is described as having been built for the most part of chalk with squares of flint regularly interspersed. Subsequently a Doric

"THE EVENING ON THE WAY."

porch was added, and a century later still the picturesque dormer windows and gables were removed, and other "restorations" effected, including the covering of the whole of the front with paint and stucco.

Meanwhile the property had been passing through various hands, ultimately becoming part of the Onslow estate. For a time it belonged to Daniel Colwall, concerning whom a few words are called for. Colwall was a man of note in his day. He was a prominent member of the Royal Society, was for a time its treasurer, and one of the founders of its museum. His end, however, was tragic. He shot himself at the Friary House, and the chair in which the deed was committed was presented by George, Earl of Onslow, to the master's apartments of Abbot's Hospital, where it can be seen, with traces of the blood-stains still upon it.

In 1794, further changes befell the Friary. Russell tells us that extensive Cavalry Barracks having been erected on the ground belonging to and surrounding the Friary, the building was fitted up and appropriated for the reception of the officers. While so used, George IV., when Prince of Wales, the Dukes of York, Cumberland and Cambridge, and Elfi Bey, the Mameluke Chief, visited and stayed in the building. In 1818 the barracks and all that remained of the Friary House built by Lord Annandale were pulled down, and the material sold by public auction. The ground was let to Mr. W. Elkins, and by his kindness was used by the public as a cricket and pleasure field. Twenty-two years later the whole site was sold by the Government, and the fine avenue of elms in front of the old house was cut down. The barrack ground, then known as Friary precinct, was soon covered with buildings, while Mr. J. Mangles, who bought much of the land, laid out a street called Friary Place. The houses on one side of the Place were afterwards taken down and rebuilt in North Street, next to the Wesleyan Chapel.

MILLMEAD.
(From a photograph by Mr. A. E. Moon.)

CHAPTER VI.

RCHBISHOP ABBOT holds a clearly defined place in the history of the English Church. He was the last of the Puritan Primates of his age, and the immediate predecessor of Laud. He fought obstinately and consistently for Protestantism and against Romanism, as he understood them both. And although in the long run he was worsted in the struggle, he was for years in the forefront of the religious life of his country and the acknowledged champion of one great school of theological thought.

The red brick Tudor building at the summit of the High Street hill, invariably spoken of locally as "Abbot's Hospital," though its correct title is "The Hospital of the Blessed Trinity," is the munificent gift Abbot designed to keep his memory green in his native town. No Guildfordian has left behind him a worthier memorial. Abbot tells us that he held it agreeably to his duty to bequeath to posterity "some monument of his thankfulness to his Creator and some testimony of his faith in Jesus Christ." For he had been, he says, "partaker of some earthly and worldly benefits, more than most of my birth and rank have attained to." A glance at the main features of his career suffices to show that this description does not exaggerate the good fortune which in so many ways assisted him in his advancement stage by stage from a very humble home in Guildford to the chair of St. Augustine.

George Abbot was born on October 29, 1562, in a small wooden cottage described as "the first house over the bridge in St. Nicholas parish." This tenement, which in 1692 was an inn known as the Three Mariners, and which was afterwards included within the precincts of Messrs. Crooke's brewery, remained standing till 1864, and was, unhappily, then demolished. George was the second of six sons born in this dwelling. His father, Maurice Abbot, was a clothworker who had been married at St. Mary's Church in 1548 to Alice March. Both parents were staunch Protestants and had endured persecution. Maurice Abbot suffered for his steadfastness in the Protestant religion, says Fuller, through the means of Dr. Story, "and, indeed, had Story been a Bonner, Alice for her zeal had suffered martyrdom." Fortunately they lived to see quieter and happier times. Alice Abbot, according to a well-known tradition, was the heroine of a strange vision shortly before the birth of her son George. She dreamt that if she could eat a jack or pike the expected child would be a great man. "Upon this," says Aubrey, "she was indefatigable to satisfy her longing as well as her dream. She first inquired out for this fish, but accidentally taking up some of the river water that runs close to the

ABBOT'S BIRTHPLACE
(*From an old print.*)

house in a pail, she took up the much-desired dainty, dressed it, and devoured it almost all."

Yet another tradition is connected with the boy's early days. "As he and his brother," says Russell, "were playing on the bridge, some gentlemen passing were struck by their appearance, and being informed that one of these was the subject of this remarkable dream, they ordered them directly to school, and maintained them while there and afterwards at the University."

Whether or not some benefactor thus intervened, George Abbot, with his brothers Robert and Maurice, began his education in the Guildford Grammar School some twenty years after the school had received its charter from

8

Edward VI.   The Rev. Francis Taylor was headmaster at the time, and Abbot's grateful recollection of him is shown in the fact that one of his first appointments as Primate was to confer upon Taylor the rectory of Lambeth.

In 1578 Abbot entered Balliol College, Oxford; in 1582 he took his B.A. degree; in 1583 he was chosen probationer Fellow of his college; and in 1585 he was admitted M.A. and was ordained.   The next eight years were devoted to the study of theology and to tutorial work.   It is easy to conceive some of the influences that at this time helped to mould and strengthen the convictions which controlled his policy when, later on, he figured among the leading men of his generation.   For the thirty years which formed the first span of his life marked also the upgrowth of the new England he had subsequently to face as the seventeenth century opened.   They were years when the throne was occupied by a monarch who had inspired her subjects with a personal devotion and a passionate fervour of loyalty unequalled in English annals.   They were years when the peace and social order and progress which Elizabeth's statesmanship ensured for her subjects rendered possible the rapid growth of national commerce and sowed the seeds of future industrial greatness.   They were years when the love of travel and adventure prompted John Hawkins and Drake to voyage to the Far West and Frobisher to the Far North, and stimulated our sons of the sea to brave the Atlantic in vessels not larger than a collier's brig of to-day.   Still further, the wonders of the New World transfused and revivified the thought and intellect of the Old.   The influence of the Renaissance was slowly permeating English intellectual life, and the way was being paved for the ever memorable outburst of literary activity in which the names of Marlowe, Spenser, Bacon, and Shakespeare were afterwards conspicuously to figure.

Not less momentous was the moral and religious movement of the time. When Elizabeth came to the throne three-fourths of her subjects were Catholic. At her death Romanism was vigorous only in the North and in the extreme West.   Apart from the literary revival already touched upon, the steady efforts of the Queen and her ministers to stamp out recusancy and to enforce conformity were of course largely instrumental in bringing about this change.   But the developments of international politics operated in the same direction, and the defeat of the Armada fixed once and for all the position of England as a Protestant nation, strong enough and self-reliant enough to grapple victoriously with the most potent forces the Pope could then command.

Abbot had been four years a Fellow at Balliol when Elizabeth's sailors thus crushed the designs of the Spaniards.   His surroundings at Oxford were quite in harmony with the staunch Protestantism in which he had been born and bred.   True, the University was termed a nest of Papists at the beginning of the reign, but before Elizabeth passed away it was "a hotbed of Puritanism, where the fiercest tenets of Calvin reigned supreme" (J. R. Green). We know little of Abbot's earlier work at Oxford from 1583 to 1591, but in the latter year he received his first mark of favour from one to whom he afterwards owed much. Lord Buckhurst, a strong Puritan, was in 1591 appointed Chancellor of the University, and nominated Abbot as his private chaplain. The connection so begun lasted till Buckhurst's death, and in the dedication of his lectures on Jonah, Abbot very frankly and gratefully acknowledges the benefits he owed to his patron. These lectures on Jonah, which were not published until 1600, are the chief fruit that now remains of Abbot's labours during the closing years of the century. They were delivered, he tells us, at intervals of four or five years, "both winter and summer, on Thursday mornings early." They are an

ABBOT'S BIRTHPLACE.
(Originally drawn for Russell's "History of Guildford.")

exhaustive exposition of Jonah's life and prophecies, with many digressions on current affairs. Two years before "Jonah" saw the light Abbot also published a volume in Latin dealing with six theological questions, then under discussion at Oxford. These essays were reprinted in Germany in 1610.

Meanwhile Buckhurst's influence was successfully exerted on his protégé's behalf. In 1597 Abbot, having just taken the degree of Doctor of Divinity, was appointed Master of University College, then, according to Clarendon, one of the poorest colleges in Oxford. In 1599 he was made Dean of Winchester ; in 1600 he was nominated Vice-Chancellor of his University, and was re-elected to the post both in 1603 and 1605. The latter position Abbot had held but a few weeks when a curious issue was submitted to him. The citizens of London, unable themselves to solve satisfactorily the question whether the ancient cross in Cheapside, which it had been necessary to repair, should be re-erected with or without a crucifix, sought counsel from both Universities on the point. Abbot's reply was emphatic and characteristic. All symbols and images he deemed to be censurable as tending to Papistry, and he urged that a pyramid or some other merely ornamental erection, should be substituted for the crucifix. It was of course precisely on this principle that Abbot acted in Oxford itself when he caused a number of paintings on sacred subjects to be burnt in the market place.

ARCHBISHOP ABBOT.

It can hardly be conceived, indeed, that Abbot was personally popular in the University. True, we need not accept as judicial Clarendon's description of him as " a man of very morose manners and of very sour aspect." But he was unquestionably a strict disciplinarian, and his kindlier traits were not always apparent in his dealings either with those who were under his rule, or with those who viewed life and religion from a standpoint other than his own. It is

ABBOT'S TOMB, HOLY TRINITY CHURCH, GUILDFORD.

perhaps significant that on one occasion during his third term of office no less than 140 undergraduates were sent to prison for disrespectfully sitting with their hats on in St. Mary's Church. On the other hand, Abbot clearly won the gratitude of many of his pupils. One of them, Sir Dudley Digges, in after life still spoke of him as "father." Another, Sir George Savile, left his son to Abbot's guardianship.

Much graver matters than infractions of University discipline were, however, soon to engage Abbot's attention. As the seventeenth century opened, the first portents of the coming struggle with Arminianism began to manifest themselves. Laud was appearing on the scene, and soon he and Abbot were in conflict. As a divinity lecturer at St. John's, Oxford, Laud had asserted the perpetual visibility of "the Church of Christ, derived from the Apostles and the Church of Rome, continued in that Church, and in others of the East and South through the Reformation." Abbot promptly accepted the challenge thus thrown out. He rebuked Laud, and drew up a summary of his own views on the subject, in which he emphatically denied "that the Bishop of Rome and his pontifical clergy should have the face of the Church tied and inseparably joined unto them." This treatise was not published at the time : but, somewhat unfortunately for Abbot, saw the light twenty years later through the excessive zeal of an anonymous friend, when Laud and his co-workers were fast gaining the upper hand. Abbot's influence, again, is alleged to have been responsible for the reprimand openly administered to Laud in 1606 " for sundry scandalous and Popish passages in a sermon at St. Mary's." These incidents, as subsequent events very plainly show, were but the beginning of a feud which lasted till Abbot's death, and the echoes of which have quite recently sounded again in our ears. Meanwhile, it is pleasanter, as Mr. Sydney Lee has said, to think of Abbot as busily occupied with an important share in the preparation of the authorized version of the Bible. He was one of the divines to whom James entrusted this task, and, with seven other Oxford graduates, he revised the four Gospels, the Acts, and the Apocalypse. Mention should be made here, too, of his small volume entitled ".A Brief Description of the Whole World," published in 1600. The work clearly hit the taste of the day, for it ran through many editions, and its issue indicates that Abbot was alive to the thirst for information concerning other lands which sprang out of the love of travel and adventure so characteristic of the time.

A decisive turning-point in Abbot's life was reached in 1608. By the death of Lord Buckhurst he lost his first patron. He was soon, however, to find a still more influential friend in George Hume, Earl of Dunbar, who was then high in the favour of James. Abbot accompanied Dunbar to Scotland, with a view to bringing about the restoration of the Episcopacy north of the Tweed, and the mission appears to have been in a measure successful, since it led to the appointment of a number of bishops as "constant moderators" to their presbyteries. Abbot, however, turned this Scotch journey to account in another direction. While he was in the North, public attention was centred in the trial and execution of George Sprot, for participation in, or knowledge of the Gowrie conspiracy. An account of Sprot's trial was published by Sir William Hart, the judge before whom he was arraigned. To this composition Abbot contributed a lengthy introduction, in which, with fulsome flattery, James was compared to David, Solomon, Moses, and Constantine, and the monarch's

ABBOT'S HOSPITAL.

life was asserted to be "so immaculate and unspotted in the world, that even malice itself could not find true blemish in it."

Whatever motive may have inspired this absurd panegyric, Abbot was soon to have an opportunity of forming a juster estimate of the King's wisdom and spotless virtue. For promotion followed quickly on his return from Scotland. In December, 1609, he was appointed Bishop of Lichfield and Coventry, only to be translated to the See of London in the following year ; and on the death of

Bancroft, at the begianing of 1611, the summit of his ambition was reached by his preferment to the Primacy.

Of this last promotion Abbot had no hopes. He had already risen fast and high : Dunbar, his patron and friend at Court, was dead. But, as a matter of fact. Dunbar had done his work. Before he died, his counsel in the matter had been tendered to the King, and ultimately swayed the latter's choice.

When the news came Abbot was " wonderstruck." " Preferment did fly upon him," says Fuller, " without his expectations." But the appointment was far from popular. Laud and his school were loud in their disapproval and disappointment. Others, although more in harmony with Abbot's theological views, nevertheless felt and urged that the new Archbishop had had no parochial training, and knew nothing of the sufferings of the lower clergy. Others yet again held that Abbot was lacking in the broad and tolerant statesmanship imperatively called for by the circumstances of the Church at that juncture. Still, in some respects Abbot entered upon his high position under favourable conditions. If he had enemies at Court, like Rochester, he had also many staunch friends among the officers of State. If Laud and his supporters still breathed hostility and defiance, Abbot enjoyed the goodwill and confidence of the King. The Queen was cordially disposed towards him, and the young Prince Henry venerated him. In a word, although some serious difficulties were plainly besetting his path, he had a tolerably fair field before him, and there was much friendly and powerful influence that he could summon to his aid.

In a brief review such as this, I must necessarily refrain from reference in any detail to many points of interest which marked Abbot's strong and active rule as Primate. I can say nothing of his quarrel with Coke, his relations with Bacon, his attitude in connection with the trial of Raleigh. I cannot touch upon the characteristic desire of the man who, rugged and stern as he seemed to the world and his opponents, had yet a large and generous heart, to show his gratitude to his Alma Mater by constant efforts to improve her government, and by liberal gifts towards new buildings within her boundaries. I must content myself with noting briefly the main lines of his policy, and the more prominent transactions in which he figured. However seriously we estimate Abbot's shortcomings, one strongly-marked virtue must at least be accredited to him. His aims and views were consistent throughout. If and when he erred in judgment on some of the graver issues which came before him, the error did not arise from the weakness of vacillation. It is to be explained by the narrowness of his vision, by the dominating power of the beliefs and influences which had surrounded his childhood and moulded his youth and manhood, and were to colour and limit his outlook on life until his course was run. Abbot always knew his own mind; but it was his fate to live in times when the whole temper of religious thought was moving rapidly in a direction different from his own. Rigidly adhering to the convictions which at Oxford had brought him into conflict with Laud, he was resolved as Primate to do his utmost, both at home and abroad, to fight Rome in whatever guise she seemed to him to threaten or attack the reformed faith. He recognised no middle course; strenuous and unsparing opposition to Romish doctrines and usages, and to all who would spread or revive them, was to him both the right and the only defensible

INTERIOR OF BOARD ROOM, ABBOT'S HOSPITAL.

attitude. Hence in 1615 a renewal of hostilities with Laud; hence, too, the persistent persecution and imprisonment of recusants which unhappily marked his rule.

On the other hand, Abbot had no sympathy with extreme Puritanism. "He connived to a limited extent," says Hallam, "at some irregularities of the Puritanical clergy, judging not absurdly that their scruples at a few ceremonies, which had been aggravated by a vexatious rigour, would die away by degrees." But he strongly upheld the Episcopacy as a superintending pastorate; he believed in obedience to the Crown and all duly constituted authority, and to the last he strove to secure conformity to the Church, and showed his innate love of order. It is no small praise, too, to say of Abbot that, despite the character of the Court in which he moved, he resolutely upheld the sanctity of the marriage tie.

The worst blot on Abbot's record as Archbishop sprang from his unfailing disposition to condemn, as either Romanist or atheistical, all the newer doctrines which the intellectual and religious awakening of his age brought to the front. In March, 1612, Bartholomew Legate was burned at Smithfield as an obstinate Arian heretic; in April of the same year Edward Wyghtman, who was charged with "entertaining the errors of ten Hæresiarchs," suffered a similar fate at Lichfield. James himself was principally responsible for this revival of the infamous cruelties of earlier days; but Abbot, unhappily, was far from blameless. The Egerton papers afford indisputable evidence that the Archbishop wrote to Lord Ellesmere, as Lord Chancellor, to secure the choice of judges—carefully excluding Coke—who could be counted upon to do the King's will in the matter of these " two blasphemous heretics."

Fortunately for his reputation, Abbot was not always thus pliable to the King's pleasure. When James attempted, in 1613, to divert to his own uses the Sutton bequests to the Charterhouse, Abbot strongly opposed the monarch's design, and ultimately won the day. Still wider was the breach between the two with regard to the divorce of the Countess of Essex. Abbot twice or thrice on his knees besought the King to dispense with his services as president of the Commission which was to hear this cause. But the King was obdurate, and Abbot, thus compelled to make his choice, held his ground with characteristic courage, and pronounced definitely in favour of the validity of the marriage, although seven out of twelve Commissioners took the opposite view, and granted the Countess's suit. One contemporary chronicler gravely ascribes all Abbot's subsequent misfortunes to his disregard of the King's wishes in this matter. But it must be added that some reconciliation seems to have been effected, for the Primate was present at the marriage of the Countess with Somerset in 1614.

In one effort he made in the following year to strengthen his position at Court, Abbot was particularly unhappy. He could hardly have taken a more disastrous step than that by which he brought George Villiers to the notice of the King. True, the two men were then on the most affectionate terms. Villiers styled the Primate " Father," and Abbot in return declared that he would repute and esteem him as his son. But the Queen judged Villiers' character only too accurately when she told the Archbishop that the first person this young man would plague would be the friend who thus laboured for his promotion. Her prediction was quickly verified. Villiers had no sooner gained the ear of the King than the project of a Spanish marriage was revived, to be persistently championed by Abbot's old foe, Laud. Years before, Abbot had vehemently opposed the proposal to betroth Prince Henry to a Spanish Princess. Now that Henry was dead, he was not a whit more favourably disposed towards the suggested alliance of Charles with the Spanish Court. When, after fruitless opposition in conjunction with the Commons, he signed the articles of the suggested marriage treaty (July, 1623), he did so only on receiving orders under the Great Seal. His satisfaction knew no bounds at the news of the failure of the negotiations, and he joyfully met the young Prince on his arrival from Spain in London at Lambeth Stairs, and had him conveyed in his own barge to York House.

Abbot's influence was much more successfully exerted on behalf of the suit of the Protestant Elector Palatine for the hand of the Princess Elizabeth. To his sincere delight, and largely as a result of his own efforts, he ceremoniously affianced the young couple at Whitehall in December, 1612, and married them in the following February. But even in this connection Abbot was doomed to disappointment. When, in 1619, the Protestant Bohemians renounced their allegiance to the Emperor of Austria, and chose the Elector as their King, James refused to recognise the new monarch. Further, when the German princes espoused the cause of Bohemia, James not only withheld all aid, but threatened war against Holland, the one Power which was in earnest in the Palatine's behalf. At all this, Abbot was much distressed. Unable, through illness, to attend the Council at which the question was discussed, he wrote on his sick-bed imploring the King to strike one blow for Protestantism. But his appeal availed nothing. The King's desire for the friendship of Spain outweighed all the considerations the Primate could urge.

A little later (July 24, 1621) the tragic incident befell Abbot which did so much to darken the closing years of his life. Whilst with his host, Lord Zouche, on a hunting expedition in Bramshill Park, Abbot aimed a crossbow bolt at a buck. Unhappily, the arrow hit a park-keeper, Peter Hawkins, who had carelessly ridden between the Archbishop and the deer, and the man bled to death before help could be obtained. It was, of course, a terribly sad scene. Charles Kingsley pictured it two centuries afterwards in his own vivid style and in words which well bear quotation. He wrote (July 14, 1842) : " I went the other day to Bramshill Park, and there I saw the very tree where an ancestor of mine, Archbishop Abbot, in James First's time, shot the keeper by accident. I sat under the tree, and it all seemed to me like present reality. I could fancy the noble old man, very different then from his picture

as it hangs in our dining-room at Chelsea.* I could fancy the deer sweeping
by, and the rattle of the crossbow, and the white splinters sparkling off the
fated tree as the bolt glanced and turned, and then the death shriek and the
stagger and the heavy fall of the sturdy forester, and the bow dropping from
the old man's hands, and the blood sinking to his heart in one chilling rush,
and his glorious features collapsing into that look of changeless and rigid
sorrow which haunted me in the portrait upon the wall in childhood.   He never
smiled again."

Abbot's grief and remorse were indeed extreme.   He settled an annuity
of £20 on the widow—who soon found another husband—and for the rest
of his life observed a monthly fast on Tuesday, the day of the week on which
the fatality happened.   But the affair naturally created much noise.   James,
to his credit be it said, showed common-sense and sympathy.   "An angel
might have miscarried in this sort," is reported to have been his verdict on
the narrative as it reached him.   But Abbot's enemies, and especially those
within the Church, were quick to seize their opportunity.   Williams and Laud
declared that, as the Archbishop had been guilty of "homicide," he could not,
under Canon Law, continue to discharge his functions as Primate.   The matter
was pushed to such an extreme that the opinion of foreign universities was
sought on the point, and a court of inquiry instituted by the King to determine
what penalties, if any, the accident had brought in its train.   The composition
of this Commission shows how strong were the forces at work against Abbot
at this time.   For, of its ten members, three were Bishops-elect—Laud,
Williams and Cary—who were known to be hostile to the Primate.   Moreover,
Abbot's very natural request to be represented by counsel was refused when
the Commission set to work.   In the long run, a halting decision was the
outcome of the investigation, and this James had the good sense to interpret
in Abbot's favour, although it was thought advisable to grant a formal pardon
and dispensation.

Abbot felt these indignities keenly, and never quite recovered.   His power,
in fact, had almost gone.   In 1623 he retired from the Court for a time.   And
though he was called to the death-bed of James, and administered to him the
last rites and consolations of the Church, and took a leading part in the coronation of Charles, his influence was no longer paramount.   The new King was a
friend of Buckingham, and in the hands of Laud.   Abbot soon discovered that
the foes he had fought so long and so strenuously had gained the upper hand.
When Sibthorpe preached, in harmony with the views of the Court, that the
King might take his subjects' money at his pleasure, and that no one might

* See page 44.

demur to his demand on penalty of damnation, Abbot refused to license the sermon. Thereupon he was ordered to retire from Court, and his duties were entrusted to a Commission of five Bishops, among whom was Laud. The fact that this step was largely due to Villiers (now Duke of Buckingham), naturally gave an added bitterness to the blow. A year later Abbot was reinstated in his office ; but he can no longer be deemed a force in either Church or State. His life-work was practically closed.

Upon the remaining incidents of his career it is not needful to dwell. But a few words must be added with respect to the practical forms in which Abbot showed his interest in his native town. In 1614 he wrote to the Mayor to urge

ROBERT ABBOT, BISHOP OF SALISBURY.
(From an old print.)

that steps should be taken to revive the town's manufacture of woollen cloth, then seriously declining. The Archbishop suggested the "making of broad cloths, either blewes or mingled, as a likelier trade to thrive than that heretofore used." And he forwarded £100 to be distributed in bestowing "four or five pound upon every man that will sett up a loome at first." Some years subsequently, he returned to the same subject, and notified to the Mayor a gift of "one hundred pounds a year of land," to "sett up some manufacture for the ymployment of those that are younge." After his death an attempt was made to carry out this design, but with no success, and the income from his gift was ultimately applied partly to increase the funds of the Blue Coat School originated by Thomas Baker, and now known as Abbot's School, and conducted in premises at the rear of the Hospital, and partly to augment the revenues of the noble institution for the aged poor which Abbot had meanwhile founded.

The latter scheme was foreshadowed by Abbot in the first letter referred to above, in which he expressed the desire to emulate the example of his predecessor Whitgift at Croydon. It was not until 1619, however, that he was able to gratify this desire. In April of that year he laid the first stone of the building, which was completed by 1622. A charter of incorporation was obtained from James: Richard Abbot, the Primate's eldest brother, was appointed the first master, and Abbot gave an endowment calculated to produce £300 a year. The statutes he drew up for the government of the institution provide that the inmates must be unmarried persons of not less than sixty years of age, born in Guildford or resident there twenty years. Benefactions from various donors have added to the revenues of the institution, and some changes have from time to time been made in the governing body. It is now under the control of thirteen Governors, and the growth of the endowment enables a weekly allowance of eight shillings each to be paid to twenty-two inmates to supplement the gift of a blue cloth cloak every two years and the free lodging and fuel and light to which they are also entitled.

Twenty-seven years ago the fabric of the Hospital underwent thorough repair, and among the features of interest which specially claim the visitor's attention to-day may be mentioned the fine old glass in the Chapel windows (referred to in connection with the demolition of the old Friary); the portraits, including one of Abbot himself, in the Chapel; the very fine oak panelling in the Board-room and other apartments; the handsome staircase in the master's house; and the strong-room in the tower, where the Duke of Monmouth was lodged on his way to London after the defeat at Sedgemoor.

On August 4, 1633, Abbot's long, notable and essentially strenuous career reached its close. He died at his palace at Croydon, and in compliance with his own expressed desire, and amid many manifestations of grief and respect, he was laid to rest within the walls of Holy Trinity Church. The High Street was draped in black, and Laud himself was among those who attended to pay a last tribute to the dead prelate. The handsome monument, with its finely sculptured figure of the Archbishop, which now stands in the south transept of the Church, was erected a few years after the Primate's death by his brother Maurice, and the Latin inscriptions it bears dilate upon the career and character of the deceased in a style which the custom and taste of the time no doubt approved. Posterity, of course, has judged Abbot in a very different spirit. On the one hand, he has been condemned for his morose manners, his cold and stern Puritanism, his "total ignorance of the true constitution of the Church of England," his complete failure to recognise her real place or her full mission. On the other, he has been eulogized for his wonderful temper and moderation, his sincere personal piety, his munificence to the poor and needy. Enough has been said in the foregoing pages to show in what direction the truth lies. Abbot had his strong, unwavering prejudices, and his obvious limitations of judgment ; he sometimes succumbed to the temptations inevitably attaching to both a desire for and the possession of power. But, with all shortcomings, his was a strong, virile character. His religion was firmly rooted and sincere ; his generosity was great in quarters where his sympathies were aroused ; and to the last he fought fearlessly for the form of faith he had imbibed in childhood, had taught in his early manhood, and had striven to enforce when place and power marked the summit of his career.

A few words are called for concerning two of the Archbishop's brothers. Robert Abbot claims notice from the fact that he also attained high rank in the Church. A popular preacher in his day, he became Chaplain-in-Ordinary to King James, Master of Balliol, and Regius Professor of Divinity at Oxford, and finally Bishop of Salisbury. The last piece of preferment is alleged to have been due to his vindication of the supremacy of the temporal sovereignty. In other respects, Robert seems to have shared his brother's convictions. For one of his efforts which first gained him royal favour was an elaborate dissertation to establish the identity of the Church of Rome with the Antichrist of the Apocalypse. Both at Oxford and at Salisbury, moreover, he was a vigorous exponent of Calvinism. The contrast Fuller has drawn between the two prelates has often been quoted. "George was the more plausible preacher, Robert the greater scholar ; George the abler statesman, Robert the deeper divine ; gravity did frown in George, and smile in Robert."

Maurice Abbot won position and fame in a different sphere. He was an eminently successful City merchant who amassed wealth, enjoyed the respect of his fellow-citizens, and received special marks of royal favour. One of the early directors of the East India Company, he was knighted by Charles soon after the latter's accession, represented the City of London in Parliament in 1625 ; was appointed Sheriff in 1627, and Lord Mayor in 1638. He died in 1640. The fact that he was sent with Sir Dudley Digges to Holland to effect arrangements with the Dutch monopolists in connection with the seizure of British goods in the Eastern seas, may be taken to indicate the confidence reposed in his judgment and ability.

CHAPTER VII

HE Grammar School of Guildford boasts an earlier origin than most of the foundations with which the name of Edward VI. is associated. It owed its origin to private rather than regal generosity, some forty years before that monarch came to the throne. But of its original benefactor, Robert Beckingham, we now know little, save that he was a citizen and grocer of the City of London and owned property in Guildford. During his lifetime he gave to the Mayor and approved men a house and tenement near the Castle ditch for erecting and maintaining a free school in the borough, and at his death in 1509 he bequeathed for the same purpose a rent-charge upon lands at Bromley, Kent, and Newington, Surrey. In due course his gifts were turned to account. The Mayor and approved men in 1520 provided a site for the school on land close to the tenement presented by Beckingham in the Castle ditch, and here, on the spot, it has been surmised, now occupied by the Public Baths, the town's free school was first started. A further benefaction of two houses in St. Mary's parish followed in 1550 from Henry Polstead. Nevertheless, the school was proving a heavy charge upon the borough, and the Corporation keenly desired to obtain further assistance for it. They found their opportunity in Edward VI.'s interest in education, and his disposition to apply in this direction some of the wealth placed at his disposal by his father's suppression of the religious houses. Accordingly, with the aid of the Marquis of Northampton, then residing at the Royal Manor House in Guildford Park, and of Sir William More, of Loseley, they placed their suit before the King, urging, doubtless, that Guildford had some claim to consideration, in view of the surrender of the Friary in the previous reign.

Their prayer was granted, and they obtained (1552-53) the royal charter

EXTERIOR (SOUTH) OF THE GRAMMAR SCHOOL, BEFORE RESTORATION.
(From a photograph by Mr. G. J. Jacobs.)

they sought for, with rent-charges amounting to some £20 annually, which were formerly the property of chantries at Stoke d'Abernon and Southwell. The Mayor and approved men, the warden of the King's manor, and the Bishop of Winchester were associated by the charter in the government of the school.

In 1555 the present site of the school was secured, and in 1557 the Corporation, "at their own costs, began the large room, now the schole house, with the great chamber and garrett over the same." But progress was slow, for funds were still scarce, despite small benefactions from various sources. In 1569 John Austen, one of many Mayors of Guildford who helped the school in its early days, finding that the master and the usher lacked rooms, built the master's lodging. The cost was in part defrayed by gifts amounting to £106 from neighbouring county magnates. But Austen's son tells us that his father was "out of purse above £40," having erected "a strong and faier building of three storyes high." In 1571 William Hammond, who was thrice Mayor of the town and long one of its representatives in Parliament, and whose tomb is in Holy Trinity Church, built the usher's lodging and a gallery. Thus John Austen and William Hammond had set out the quadrangle as we know it now. But neither of them lived to finish the work. In 1581 Simon Tally, vintner, supplied the woodwork needed for the usher's lodging, and in the next year Robert Brodbridge glazed all the windows. It was left, however, for George Austen, son of John Austen, to complete the west wing begun by his father. With the aid of subscriptions from Sir William More and other county gentlemen, he accomplished this task in 1586, and at the same time converted into a library the gallery which connects the two wings and completes the street-front.

Such was the gradual growth of the school building. But it was not till 1608 that the statutes for governing its administration were settled and signed by the then Bishop of Winchester, Thomas Bilson. These statutes provided that there should be a resident master and usher, that the scholars should not exceed one hundred in number, and should be taught both Greek and Latin. Every boy was to pay one penny quarterly towards the provision of brooms and rods, and fourpence at Michaelmas for buying "clean waxen candles." The scholars of the first four forms were always to use the Latin tongue, except when permitted to do otherwise by the master; and every Saturday they were to be instructed in the principles of the Christian religion.

Thus an important change was effected in the character of the school. Beckingham, the original founder, had provided that thirty of the "poorest men's sons" of Guildford should be taught to read and write English and cast accounts perfectly, so that they should be fitted for apprentices. Under the statutes of 1608 the school took rank with the other grammar schools of the country, and this character it retained for more than a couple of centuries. The statutes, signed by Bilson, remained in force until 1835, when the Municipal Corporations Act transferred the management of the school from the Mayor and Corporation to a new body of trustees. Most of the old regulations were renewed, but the number of free scholars was reduced to ten.

The history of the school during this period need not be traced in detail. At times it fared badly, for the endowment was always inadequate, the buildings were neglected, and public interest in the foundation sank to a very low ebb. Occasionally, as during Dr. Merriman's term of office (1859-1874) a vigorous and capable headmaster secured a gratifying measure of educational efficiency and success. But after Dr. Merriman's departure matters grew worse and worse, and at length, in 1885, the Charity Commissioners intervened. Various schemes to meet the needs of the situation were suggested, such as the use for the purposes of the school of a portion of the reserve fund of the Poyle Charity, or amalgamation with Archbishop Abbot's School. But none of these suggestions met with general approval, and one or two of them aroused violent opposition. Finally, thanks to the initiative of the Rev. Canon Valpy, the munificent generosity of Mr. T. W. Powell, who contributed £1,000, the energetic action of a representative committee, of which Mr. F. Lasham and Mr. G. C. Williamson were hon. secretaries, and the hearty co-operation of many "old boys," the financial difficulties were removed, a fund of £2,240 was raised to cover the cost of urgent alterations and repairs in the old school buildings, and ultimately a scheme was formulated which won general acceptance among the townspeople, and was sanctioned by the Charity Commissioners. By this scheme the school was placed upon the basis of a town day school, giving a sound modern education, and its management was entrusted to a representative board of governors. The ex-officio members of this Board are the High Steward and the Mayor of the borough, and the Chairman of the School Board. The representative governors are nominated by the Bishop of Winchester, who of course no longer retains the direction of the religious training of the boys which the old statutes assigned to him, the Town Council and the trustees of the municipal charities. There are in addition six co-optative governors. By a subsequent arrangement the Surrey County Council also nominates two governors in view of its valuable co-operation with the school's work under the Council's technical education scheme.

The new governing body met for the first time in January, 1889, and elected Canon Valpy as its first chairman. Mr. J. C. Honeybourne, M.A., was appointed headmaster, and the work of restoring the old building was taken in hand. This work was most carefully and successfully carried out under the supervision of Mr. E. L. Lunn, the necessary external repairs were judiciously executed, and the High Street frontage retains to-day all the chief features which distinguished it many years ago. Internally the principal change has been the provision on the first floor of a light, lofty, and picturesque schoolroom, by the conversion for this purpose of the old dining-room and the removal of the dormitory, which, with its quaint cubicles, was formerly above. A portion of the old schoolroom on the ground-floor has been incorporated in the head-master's dining-room, but otherwise this room remains to a large extent in its original condition. During the progress of the work several old windows and fireplaces were opened out; the fine carved oak panelling has been repaired and the quad repaved.

THE SCHOOLROOM.

Very gratifying success has so far attended the working of the new scheme. The pupils again exceed a hundred, the valuable aid extended by the County Council has greatly strengthened the science teaching, and permitted the provision of an excellent laboratory. And the Merriman memorial medals, and the challenge medal presented by the Rev. Dr. Batterson, U.S.A., are indications of the interest which has been rekindled in the school's welfare.

If, indeed, the school's future, as there seems every reason to hope, should prove well worthy of its past, all who helped to secure for it this fresh lease of life will have cause for congratulation. For, despite all the drawbacks and

financial difficulties of the old days, the roll of the Guildford Grammar School
can boast of not a few distinguished names.   In the first century of its history it
was responsible for the training of the three Abbots —Robert, Bishop of Salisbury;

INTERIOR OF THE GRAMMAR SCHOOL, 1895.

George, Archbishop of Canterbury; and Maurice, Lord Mayor of London—
Robert Horne, Bishop of Winchester; John Parkhurst and Henry Cotton,
Bishops of Norwich; William Cotton, Bishop of Exeter; and Robert Parkhurst,

Lord Mayor of London. In later years Arthur Onslow, John Russell, R.A., Dr. Richard Valpy, Dr. Mackenzie (one of the first Bishops of Zululand), and Sir George Grey, ex-Premier of New Zealand, received at least the groundwork of their education beneath its roof.

To one of these old boys the school was indebted for the foundation of its library. John Parkhurst in 1574 bequeathed his Latin books of divinity to the service of the school of the town. The Bishop's executors were loath to carry out his instructions, and it was only after much difficulty and litigation that some of the volumes were obtained and safely brought to the Guildford School. Other donations followed, and for a time due care was taken of these treasures, a large number of the books being chained in accordance with the custom of the day. In 1648 Mr. Arthur Onslow gave eight oaks as materials for new bookshelves, and during this and the following century the library was well cared for, and enriched by many further gifts. Unhappily this state of things was not maintained in later years. The day came when, as Mr. J. Willis Clark has said, " The books were evidently looked upon as so many white elephants that could not be got rid of, but for which it was somewhat onerous to provide a stable. No definite abiding-place was assigned to them, but they were put as a measure of security first in one room and then in another, and at one period even under the floor of the principal schoolroom. Their number, which at one time must have been considerable, probably became less at each removal, and it may have been on one of these occasions that the most valuable of all, a priceless Caxton, disappeared altogether." The collection, however, still numbers over 400 volumes, of which thirty retain their chains, and all are now being carefully warehoused. Almost, if not quite, unique among the Grammar Schools of the country in the possession of a chained library, the Guildford School has an obvious duty to turn its treasures to better account than has been the case of late years.

CHAPTER VIII.

OHN RUSSELL. R.A., of whom some mention has been made in previous chapters, and examples of whose works are to be seen in the Town Hall and the Guildford and Working Men's Institute, was unquestionably one of the leading portrait-painters of his day, and held a unique position in one branch of English art.

Of his known works, amounting to nearly 1,000, a large number of specimens still extant strikingly vindicate his title to exceptional genius and almost unrivalled mastery of the medium which he made specially his own. Yet, until quite recently, Russell was little more than a name to the art world generally ; and Guildfordians, while proud to claim him as the "Guildford R.A.," could say little more of his career than that he was the most distinguished member of a family long and honourably linked with the town's history.

Thanks to the labours of another Guildfordian (Mr. G. C. Williamson) all this is now changed. An exhibition of Russell's works at Kensington in May, 1894, was a revelation of Russell's powers which surprised and impressed all who saw it. It was followed later in the year by the publication of a complete biography.* In this volume the full story of his life was told for the first time, and exquisite reproductions of many of the artist's best productions convey some idea to the present generation of the skill which won him fame a century ago.

John Russell was born in Guildford on March 29, 1745. Of his boyhood we know little, save that he was educated at the Grammar School, and that on one occasion he climbed up the then incomplete tower of Holy Trinity Church "with a bit of chalk in his mouth, to see if he could not set a mark against the top." He duly set his mark upon the brickwork within a few inches of the top,

* "John Russell, R.A.," by G. C. Williamson, with introduction by Lord Ronald Gower. London : Bell and Sons.

and on descending was rewarded for his reckless daring with a sound thrashing from his father, who had meanwhile arrived on the scene. His love for art, stimulated no doubt to some extent by the tastes of other members of the family, was manifested early. When in London, at the age of thirteen, he was presented with an etching which had caught his eye in a print-shop. Again and again, while still a youth, Russell copied this etching with careful accuracy. And a wise and fitting choice was clearly made when a little later on Russell's father placed him under the tuition of Francis Cotes, R.A., a pastellist and portrait-

RUSSELL'S BIRTHPLACE, 32, HIGH STREET.*
(From a water colour by the Artist.)

painter then at the height of his fame. How long this tutelage lasted Mr. Williamson is unable to say. But in 1767 Russell was practising on his own account, though often visiting Cotes, and it seems clear that despite the religious disputations, of which I shall have something to say hereafter, a warm friendship existed between pupil and master till the latter's death.

Shortly after leaving Cotes, Russell journeyed to Cowdray House (Midhurst) to execute his first country mission. Returning to Guildford, he

* All the illustrations in this chapter are reproduced by kind permission of Mr. G. C. Williamson from his " Life of Russell" (Geo. Bell and Sons)

had plenty of work, the Rev. C. Burdett, Rector of Holy Trinity, and Mr. and Mrs. Onslow being among those who sat to him. Subsequently, on taking up his abode in London, he was equally fortunate, and Wesley, Whitfield, and Dr. Dodd were among his patrons. Meanwhile Russell was introduced to Selina, Countess of Huntingdon, with whose strongly-marked religious views he was in many ways in close sympathy. He was urged by her to forsake his art, and join the training college she had just founded at Trevecca in Wales. This undoubtedly was a turning-point in Russell's life ; and bearing in mind his peculiar temperament, and his almost fanatical devotion to the evangelical

JOHN RUSSELL, MAYOR OF GUILDFORD, FATHER OF J. RUSSELL, R.A., 1797.

revival, the choice he was asked to make must have caused him much inward conflict. Happily for his own fame, he decided to give his natural talent free play, helped no doubt to this resolution by the fact that he was about to marry. His bride was Miss Hannah Faden, and the marriage took place on February 5, 1770.

He continued to give much time to the study of his profession. He was a student at the Royal Academy, and nine months after his marriage won the gold medal for figure drawing. Two years afterwards he was elected A.R.A. ; and it was of course to his close connection with this body that Russell owed his friendship with Sir Joshua Reynolds. But, though unmistakably making headway in his profession, and enjoying from time to time a fair amount of patronage, he was much harassed by financial troubles at this period of his career. He writes in his diary, January, 1772: "I have no money to keep myself and family;" in October, 1773, "So poor cannot afford a pair of shoes, and expenses are £300 a year;" in November of the same year, "Not a shilling in the house;" in March, 1774, "Nothing but a jail before my eyes." Timely relief came, and the pressure was relieved. A gap in the diary leaves us in ignorance of the ups and downs of the next three years. In 1779 and 1780,

MRS. RUSSELL (née PARVISH), WIFE OF JOHN RUSSELL.

however, Russell was again in low water. His diary, August, 1780, says, "In indifferent health, plagued in business, nothing but trouble, a wife and four children, and barrenness of work."

Then the tide turned, and his fame and prosperity gradually grew. In 1789 he was elected R.A., painted the portrait of the Queen, and was shortly afterwards appointed crayon portrait painter to the King and to the Prince of Wales and the Duke of York. He writes in his diary, "Though large my family, I have been able to support them in plenty. My income is above £1,000 a year, and probably on the increase."

By this time, indeed, his position was made. From now until his death he shared with Reynolds the chief portrait work of the day ; and his prices were in many cases as high as Sir Joshua's. He was, too, a prolific artist, and exhibited no less than 330 works at the Royal Academy. In 1796 he received the Royal command to execute a portrait of the Princess of Wales with the infant Princess Charlotte on her knees. The Earl of Exeter and family, Lord and Lady Onslow, Mrs. Fitzherbert, the poet Cowper, the Countess of Huntingdon, Rowland Hill, Toplady, Sheridan, Sir Joseph Banks, Sir William Herschel, are

MRS. JOHN RUSSELL (*née* FADEN), WIFE OF JOHN RUSSELL, AND HER BABY, 1774.

but a few of those who sat to him. And besides his work in London, he frequently journeyed into the country for purposes of painting, and spent much time in Shrewsbury, York, Leeds and Hull.

With advancing years came impaired health. In 1803 an attack of cholera was followed by partial deafness ; and at Hull, in 1806, he succumbed to typhus fever. His son William, afterwards Rector of Shepperton, was with him at the last, and when the end drew near, was about to pray at his bedside. The dying man raised himself, however, and stopped his son with an imperative gesture.

"No, William," said he, "do not pray for me, there is no prayer for me; from henceforth it is all praise."

The remark was quite in keeping with the artist's career. For, from the time he reached manhood, the dominating note of Russell's life and personality, apart from his artistic genius, was his intense religious feeling. His diary

informs us that he was "converted, September 30, 1764, ætat. 19, at about half an hour after seven in the evening." Ever afterwards he seems to have been haunted by an overpowering sense of his responsibility for the salvation of others, even as "brands from the burning." His persistence, I may fairly say his fanatical zeal, knew no bounds, and very often got him into difficulty. As a student he angered Cotes, his master, by his pertinacious discussion. When

executing his first commission at Cowdray House, he addressed long and
argumentative appeals to Lady Montague and her sister, despite Lord
Montague's outspoken reproof of this ill-timed proselytizing.   On his way back
to Guildford he preached "all the way to the coachman."   And in his own
house bitter quarrels arose from the same cause.   He " pronounced bitter
curses " on his mother, and denied " her being a Christian as much as the
devil himself," because she spoke " dreadful and blasphemous words against
the Old Testament."   He refused to accompany his father on a walk into the
fields on Sunday, and on another occasion declared that his parent would be
" eternally damned."   In Guildford the mob, he says, once threatened him for
preaching ; and again, "the anger of Guildford people is now arisen to that
pitch that the general expression is that they should be glad to see me with a
stone round my neck and thrown in the river."

This fervour clung to and actuated Russell till his death.   He would sit up
in a chair all night to ensure attendance at an early service.   His family prayers
were so long that cook and housemaid fell asleep on their knees.   His own
self-examination, as his diary shows, was constant and severe even to morbidness.
He attended —and freely criticised—all the preachers of his day ; and would not
willingly miss any religious excitement in the form of a special service, at which
it was at all within his power to be present.   When obliged to attend the
dinners of the Royal Academy, he withdrew early, he tells us, " because of the
filthy conversation."   And, true to his stern Puritanism, when at the zenith of
his fame the Prince Regent and a foreign ambassador were refused admission
to his studio on a Sunday, and a fashionable lady found herself rebuked by the
artist for admiring a picture of some nymphs bathing.

But it is, of course, by his art, and not by the excesses of his sincere and
deeply-rooted religious faith, that Russell's memory will be kept green.   Cotes,
Rosalba and Reynolds, Mr. Williamson holds, all influenced his style.   But in
his own distinctive branch of art he far surpassed his tutor, and the purity and
brilliance of his colouring, the strength and individuality of his portraits, place
him, as Lord Ronald Gower remarks, on a level only slightly lower than that
attained by Reynolds, Gainsborough, and Romney.

Russell, it should be added, wrote a pamphlet on the " Elements of Painting
with Crayons," besides one or two other essays, and he is said to have contributed
three short articles to the early issues of the *Evangelical Magazine*.   Later in
life, and after meeting Herschel, he devoted attention to astronomy.   For years
he spent part of his leisure in delineating a lunar map, still treasured at Oxford
Observatory ; and in 1797 he invented an apparatus which he called the
Selenographia for exhibiting the phenomena of the moon, and published a

pamphlet explanatory of it. Only three complete machines, however, were ever made.

Other members of the Russell family, whose name figures in our local annals as far back as 1509, have claims upon the gratitude of Guildfordians.

HENRY E. AUSTEN, AGED FOUR.
(From a portrait by J. Russell, R. A., owned by Lieut.-Col. and Godwin Austen, Shalford House.)

John Russell, father of the Royal Academician, and the donor of the picture in the Town Hall already referred to, was four times Mayor of the town. He was a bookseller, carrying on business in the premises in the High Street now occupied by Messrs. Stent and Sons, and was responsible for the issue of many publications of local interest and value. In 1759, as "John Russell, jun.," his name appears on the print entitled, "The North-West Prospect of Guildford,"

with smaller views of buildings surrounding it, though it is open to doubt
whether he himself drew it. In 1772 he issued the " Poetical Blossoms " of
Richard Valpy, then a youth of sixteen, and afterwards distinguished as a Greek
scholar, and great-grandfather of the present Rector of Holy Trinity and
St. Mary's. Five years later he published a life of Abbot, and—more noteworthy still –the first " History and Description of Guildford," a shilling
pamphlet of twenty-four pages. A second edition followed in 1800. It was
not, however, till 1801 that the history of the town, which is still the standard
work on the subject, came from his press. This volume, though painfully
defective in its arrangement, must always be invaluable, full as it is of carefully
compiled information, with many extracts from the original books and MSS.
of the town. Though John Russell doubtless superintended the work, it is
believed to have been written chiefly by his third son, Thomas Russell, who,
born in 1748 and dying in 1822, was for many years Rector of Clandon.

   After John Russell's death, in 1804, his business was carried on by three of
his sons. In 1845 they published the third and last edition of Russell's
" History of Guildford." This bears the imprint, " G. W. and J. Russell," and
was illustrated by woodcuts from sketches by Mr. C. C. Pyne, afterwards
drawing-master of the Grammar School. The author's name does not appear
on the title-page, but Mr. G. C. Williamson has a copy of the book bearing this
note : " The following pages were written by me at Guildford, in the beginning
of the year 1842. F. Lawrence." Lawrence was in his youth apprenticed to
the Russells. According to Brayley, he was frequently found " lost " in his
employers' circulating library, stored upstairs. Afterwards he was called to the
Bar, became an assistant in the Department of Printed Books in the British
Museum, and wrote a life of Henry Fielding.

CHAPTER IX.

I. Holy Trinity.

"TRINITY CHURCH has always been the chief of the three in Guildford, and in the old church were many things remarkable, viz., monuments."

So wrote the author of Russell's history of the town in 1801. But it must in candour be added that Holy Trinity does not to-day owe this pre-eminence to its architectural beauty. If it engages the attention of the casual visitor, the circumstance will be chiefly due to the conspicuous position the church occupies at the summit of the High Street. It must, however, also be said that, enlarged and vastly improved as it has been in recent years, the interior will far better repay inspection now than was the case a century since.

Of the foundation of the old church, to which Russell refers, and which existed till 1714, we have no record. No mention is made of it in the Domesday Book, but the advowson appears to have been given to the priory of Merton by William Testard. In its ground plan, as well as in its external features, the fabric somewhat resembles that of St. Mary's. It consisted of nave, north and south aisles, terminating eastward with apsidal chapels—the Lady Chapel and St. Nicholas, or Hammond, Chapels respectively—a chancel, square at the east end, and a low central tower surmounted by a shingled spire. Some portion of the original parsonage still remains in the cottages now standing at the south-east corner of the churchyard.

Mr. Palmer has gleaned from the pages of the vestry minute book much that is of interest concerning the old church during the last fifty years of its existence. In 1734 repairs to the chancel, which were estimated to cost £200, were found to be necessary, and apparently there was much contention as to

I 2

who should bear this outlay. Ultimately, the parishioners undertook to repair and re-pew the nave, and the sum needed for the chancel was borrowed. But Church-work in Holy Trinity parish in those good old days did not evoke either the harmony or the energy more happily associated with it now. For, four years later, the parishioners were promoting litigation against the rector, and the churchwardens against the parish clerk. And the loan of £200 was not repaid until 1755, when £168 had been paid for interest. Meanwhile, it had become manifest that the repairs under the tower had been most unwisely carried out.

HOLY TRINITY CHURCH, 1740.
(From a print in the possession of Lord Ashcombe.)

In 1740 pillars and arches were found to be fast giving way. The steeple was examined, and condemned as unsafe on April 19 ; Divine service was held in the church next day for the last time ; and on the following Wednesday, April 23, 1740, the steeple fell bodily through the roof and the nave, whilst the bells were being lowered from the tower.

The disaster appears to have had a depressing effect upon the energy of the parishioners. For the ruins were allowed to remain untouched for a couple of years, and it was not until 1751 (nine years afterwards) that the walls were finally demolished, and the first stone laid of the new building. Two years subsequently the work was stopped for want of funds, and nothing more was done till 1755. It was then decided to seek Parliamentary powers to sell the church-house and lands; and, despite the disapproval of the rector, the necessary Act was obtained. The property realized some £1,225, and at length, on September 18, 1763, twenty-three years after the disaster, the new church was first used for Divine service, which, during part of the interregnum, had been conducted in a portion of the old building.

HOLY TRINITY CHURCH, 1895.

The interior arrangement of this church is thus described by Mr. Palmer : "The three gangways from west to east," he writes. "were intersected by another, which crossed the church opposite the north door. In front of the pulpit was the Mayor and magistrates' pew, with three pews for bailiffs, an adjoining one for the Mayor and magistrates' wives, and one of great size, with a desk in the centre, for the Bishop of Winchester. Certain houses within the parish had pews allotted to them, and at the back was one for 'Serjeants' and

another for 'Livery Servants.'   In the west gallery were the seats for the
'Singers,' the Charity School, and two other schools.   Along the side-galleries
the back seats were devoted to 'maid-servants.'   'N.B.—Married women, to
whose houses no seats in particular are appropriated, are to be seated in the
side-galleries with the maid-servants.'"   An order was also issued that pews
might be lined with green, but no other colour was to be used except for those
belonging to the Bishop and Corporation.   What a charming picture this gives
of Church customs little more than a hundred years since!   In the fabric itself
there was little alteration until 1869, when the side-galleries were removed, the
windows altered, the pews lowered and re-arranged, and the organ removed
from the gallery to the east end.   The Rev. F. E. Tower, during his short
tenure of the living (1882-85), was impressed by the need for an enlargement of

the church.   But it was left to the Rev. Canon
Valpy, after Mr. Tower's death, to set on foot a
scheme which, if carried out in its complete form,
will do much more than merely provide additional
accommodation.   The first portion of this scheme
was successfully completed in 1888 under Sir Arthur
Blomfield, by the provision of a new chancel, with
north and south transepts.   The organ was removed
to the new south transept against the east wall of
which the Abbot monument was placed.   Both in
connection with and since the consecration of this
chancel, which in itself imparts to the church a
dignity and completeness it sadly lacked before, the
church has been enriched by many valuable offerings.
For example, the chancel wall-paintings include one in
memory of the Rev. F. E. Tower, which represents
St. Paul, and another of St. Augustine, commemo-
rating the episcopate of Bishop Harold Browne.

F. TILL OF HOLY TRINITY CHURCH.
(Original drawn for Russell's "History
of Guildford.")

Of the "many things remarkable, viz., monuments," which Russell mentions
as existing in the old church, but few escaped destruction in the disaster of 1740.
The handsome Abbot memorial, however, suffered no serious injury, and is in
excellent preservation.   The figure of the Primate in marble lies beneath a
rich and massive canopy, sustained by six columns of black marble, resting on
a pedestal of substantial volumes.   The canopy itself is adorned by nine small
allegorical statues of the cardinal virtues.

The cenotaph to the memory of Arthur Onslow, in the north-east corner of
the nave, fittingly commemorates a generous benefactor to the church ; brasses
recall the memory of Abbot's parents and of Henry Norbridge, several times

Mayor of Guildford, and his wife ; and the monument to Sir Robert and Lady Parkhurst, in the principal porch at the west end, reminds Guildfordians to-day of a family long prominently connected with the town.

The monuments destroyed in 1740 included one to the memory of William Hammond, who, besides his benefactions to the Grammar School, at his death in 1575 bequeathed to the churchwardens his house next above the church (No. 145, High Street) for the use and the reparation of the church, and especially of St. Nicholas' chancel, in which he desired that his body might be buried. From this gift arose the custom of terming the chapel of St. Nicholas Hammond's Chapel.

The present vestry at the south-west corner was originally a chantry chapel, founded by one of the Westons of Sutton. For years this was little else than a lumber-room, but a very laudable restoration in 1869 enabled it to be used for the purpose to which it is now put, with the consent of the family to whom it belongs, and who still exercise rights over it.

II. St. Mary's.

How full of interest the story would be if we could but trace and illustrate stage by stage the changes, the restorations, and perhaps the mutilations St. Mary's Church has undergone since the Norman columns of the nave were erected six or seven centuries ago !

But this story, of course, can never now be fully told, and we have little to help us recall the past. The oldest portions of the church date back certainly to Henry II., if not to his predecessor, and the foundation, as in the case of Holy Trinity, has been attributed to the Testards. In the early part of the reign of Henry III., the Vicar of St. Mary's "gave 40s. a year to have a fair to be held near the church for three days, till the King should be of age." But thenceforward the records are blank for many generations, although the fabric itself bears testimony to large alterations in the thirteenth, fourteenth, and fifteenth centuries. Fate was less kind in the Georgian era. Originally the east end of the chancel was semicircular, and "extended," says Russell, "into the garden of the opposite Rectory house." This was too great an inconvenience to be patiently borne by the Guildfordian of those days. In 1755, by order of the vestry, the " east churchyard wall was moved further into the churchyard, and the ground taken into the highway." In return, the parish took upon themselves "the whole repairs of the east end of the chancel next the road and the great east window, thenceforward from time to time and at all times, and for ever save the Rector and his successors from all charges concerning the same." As part of the bargain, a fine row of elms standing between the east gate of the churchyard and the corner of the south chancel was destroyed.

In 1825 a step further on the same path was taken. To widen the thoroughfare to Brighton, and—so the legend runs—for the special accommodation of George IV., who favoured this route to and from Windsor and the Sussex coast, a portion of the chancel was removed. Fortunately on this occasion some slight respect was shown to the building. The stones and carvings were marked, and the large east window, with its interesting Perpendicular tracery, was carefully replaced. Such were the relations between Church and State—in Guildford, at any rate—in the days of the Georges! And thus,

ST. MARY'S CHURCH, 1700.
From a print in the possession of Lord Ashcombe.

too, it has come about that the chancel as we see it to-day lacks due proportion, and ends almost in a line with the side chapels.

In 1863 very thorough restoration was carried out, and the church as it now stands is full of interest. The nave is separated from the aisles, one of which is three feet narrower than the other, by arches springing from Norman columns; the corbels which supported the original roof terminate in bat-winged, clawed, and dog-faced monsters; and the windows, it will be noted, vary from Early English to Perpendicular. Three steps lead from the nave to the tower, which rests on four open arches. Here, again, it is curious to observe that two of these are plainly Norman and two Early English. Four steps more lead to the chancel, whose vaulted roof is supported by Early English shafts in triple clusters. On the north side is the chapel of St. John the Baptist : on the south St. Mary's Chapel, the latter used as an organ-chamber and vestry. In both chapels are large hagioscopes piercing the wall eastward, by which worshippers in the chapel gained a view of the high altar. Moreover, during the restoration of 1863, leper windows were discovered under the west windows of both aisles, and one has since been filled with stained glass.

ST. MARY'S CHURCH, 1865.

The wall paintings in St. John the Baptist's Chapel are unquestionably the most remarkable feature of the church. They were brought to light during the alterations in 1825, whilst the workmen were engaged in scraping the whitewash from the vaulted ceiling. Since then their unique interest has been generally recognised, and much has been written concerning their origin and probable significance. Mr. J. G. Waller has discussed the subject exhaustively in an elaborate paper,* and favours the supposition that the paintings were executed

" Archæologia," vol. xlix.

by William of Florence when in Guildford to carry out work for Henry III. at the royal palace.

The designs are curious, and call for a few words of explanation. On the spandrils of the arch on the left St. Michael is to be seen weighing the merits of a human soul in the form of a naked man, whilst a winged demon endeavours with his foot to press down the ascending scale. On the opposite spandrils an angel consigns to punishment two souls, who are led off by a demoniacal figure. In the centre of the vault a medallion shows the Saviour in majesty, with the right hand raised in benediction, and the left hand holding a book or table, upon which is the Alpha and Omega. The remaining frescoes may be thus briefly indicated : (1) The Jew at Berytus, represented at the font and receiving absolution from Christ, with the figure of a scribe standing near at hand. (2) Herod receiving the executioners of St. John the Baptist, one of whom carries St. John's head on a sword. (3) Christ casting out devils, with the Syro-Phœnician woman kneeling in supplication ; a man and two menacing demons. (4) Illustrative of the legend according to which St. John drank without harm the poison offered to him by Aristodemus ; two corpses on the ground testify to the deadly character of the draught. (5) The raising of Drusiana by St. John, with illustrations also of the legendary story of Crates and St. John, and the conversions of rods and stones into gold and gems. (6) St. John is depicted in the vat of boiling oil, with Christ appearing to support and bless him.

It may be true, as Mr. Waller gives cause for thinking, that William the Florentine was an artist of only ordinary merit. But the remnants of his work at St. Mary's, faded and indistinct though they are, give a unique interest to the Church.

By an Act obtained in 1698-99, the parishes of Holy Trinity and St. Mary were united for ecclesiastical purposes only.

III. St. Nicolas.

There is certainly some warrant for the supposition that St. Nicolas can claim an older foundation than either Holy Trinity or St. Mary's. For if in Saxon days Guildford was situated for the most part on the west bank of the Wey, it is only reasonable to assume also that this community possessed a church. Of St. Mary's and Holy Trinity, however, as we have already seen, we have no trace earlier than Norman times.

Whether this be so or not, Guildfordians still living can recall three successive fabrics on the spot now occupied by the somewhat massive building on the river side close by the old bridge. The first of these Russell described in 1801 as an old church "which had undergone many alterations." "It had a round tower, said John Apark, an old inhabitant and formerly beadle of the town," he tells us in a footnote. But this round tower disappeared at the beginning of the eighteenth century, and a square tower with battlements was erected in its place. Much more than this had, however, to be done later on. For the church had been built on a morass or quagmire, and was often flooded for weeks at a time. In 1796 repairs became urgently necessary. The old pillars and arches were removed, the floor was raised some three feet, and new

ST. NICOLAS CHURCH, 1837—1875.
(From a print in the possession of Lord Ashcombe).

pews were provided. By this effort some thirty or forty years were tided over. But in 1836 more drastic measures were called for, and it was decided to pull down the old building and erect a new and larger church.

This task was accomplished in the following year, Mr. R. Ebbels being the architect. A contemporary writer somewhat verbosely describes the new church as "a tasteful and elegant fabric, constructed on the purest extant models of the best era of church architecture, in the Gothic or Pointed style." As, however, the writer goes on to admit that "the galleries encroach too much, perhaps, on

13

the area of the building, and tend to give it somewhat a confined appearance,"
we may be forgiven for thinking that some advance in taste and knowledge in
these matters has since been seen. Nevertheless, two points in connection with
Mr. Ebbels' church deserve notice. The old tower, erected a little over a
century before, was not taken down. It was strengthened, and by the addition
of new buttresses, cornices, parapets, and doorway, was made to harmonize with
Mr. Ebbels' Gothic. The Loseley Chapel was also wisely preserved and incorporated in the new building.

But with this erection the parishioners were not long content. Shortly
after Dr. Monsell, the well-known hymnologist, was presented to the benefice in
1870, a movement was set on foot to rebuild once more. Designs were prepared
for a church on a new site by Mr. S. S. Teulon. After his death they were
modified, and carried out on the original site by the late Mr. Ewan Christian, as
Mr. Teulon's executor. Unhappily the Rector himself was not permitted to see
the completion of an undertaking which owed much to his energy and tact, and
the progress of which he had watched with keen delight. For a fall he met
with while watching the building operations had fatal consequences on April 9,
1876, only a week or two before the consecration service. In the churchyard
near the vestry stands one specially interesting tribute to Dr. Monsell's memory.
It consists of the fragment of a stone column discovered in the middle of the wall
of the old tower when demolished to make room for the present erection.

The designs thus executed by Mr. Christian are massive and substantial.
Externally the effect will certainly be more pleasing when the tower is
surmounted with the timber spire shown on the original plans.* The slight
irregularity in the arrangement of the south aisle will of course be praised rather
than censured, since it permitted the retention of the Loseley Chapel. Internally,
indeed, the church has been richly, almost lavishly, beautified. The wall-
paintings of the chancel, the marble pulpit, a memorial to Bishop Hatchard,
twelve years Rector of the parish, and afterwards Bishop of Mauritius, the
memorial windows to Dr. Monsell, and the font and its carved canopy all claim
notice.

The Loseley Chapel is divided from the church by an arcade. It has been
restored by Mr. W. More-Molyneux, and contains many monuments of the
Mores of Loseley, the chief being a large altar-tomb of Sir W. More and his
wife Margaret, who died in 1600. Under the south window is the remarkable
altar-tomb (formerly in the north aisle of the old church) of Arnold Brocas, at
one time Rector of the parish. His effigy represents him in a scarlet robe,

* See *Builder*, April 29, 1876.

ST. NICOLAS CHURCH, 1817.
(From a print in the possession of Lord Edwards.)

beneath a Gothic canopy ; an angel supports his head, and his feet rest upon a dog ; an inscription gives the date of his death as 1395.

A good deal of local interest attaches also to the memorial brass to Caleb Lovejoy. The inscription tells us that Lovejoy was born in St. Nicolas parish in 1603, was educated at the Grammar School, and "before the age of fifteen was by his parents thence removed to London, where he hath neare accomplished the age of four times fifteen years more." On his death he left some property in Walnut Tree Alley, Southwark, to his native parish, for the benefit of the poor,

under an elaborate series of regulations. In one of the notes to his work on "Traders' Tokens," Mr. G. C. Williamson brings to light some interesting facts in connection with Lovejoy and his bequest. It seems that, after settling in London, Lovejoy became a successful trader, and the Exchequer Depositions in the Record Office tell us that he was waggoner to Oliver Cromwell.

Walnut Tree Alley, Mr. Williamson goes on to show, had at one time been the site of the manor house of the Warrennes. It became the house of the priors of Lewes, and was occupied after the dissolution in part by St. Olave's Grammar School, and partly by the Walnut Tree Inn. In 1757 some portion of

the Alley was used as the site of the Carter Lane Chapel, the meeting-place of
the Baptist Church, which, after a succession of removals, ultimately worshipped
under Mr. Spurgeon at the Metropolitan Tabernacle.   Curious, indeed, are the
links in the chain which thus in a degree associates this Guildfordian with one of
the chief Nonconformist places of worship in the Metropolis.

Caleb Lovejoy himself was buried in his native parish, as the quaint epitaph
on the brass informs the passer-by.

IV.   St. John the Evangelist, Stoke.

It is inaccurate, as every Guildfordian is aware, to classify St. John the
Evangelist, Stoke, with the town churches.   For though of late years Guildford
has rapidly absorbed those portions of this large parish which were nearest to
the municipal boundaries, " Old Stoke Church " still lies outside the borough,
and retains most of the characteristics of a village church.   A somewhat
rambling, Perpendicular building, with a picturesque ivy-clad tower, it stands
in a corner of Stoke Park as an outpost of rural territory fast yielding to
invasion by the inhabitants of the adjacent town.   Nevertheless, it will be convenient to include in this chapter the few words that have to be said concerning
the history of the fabric and the local associations which cluster around it.

It is impossible now to discern any traces of the church which existed in
Stoke when the Domesday Survey was made.   Moreover, much has been done
during the present century to transform the interior and modify some of the
external features of the existing church.   Enlargement has been necessary
from time to time ; the south porch has been converted into a vestry-room, and
a new porch added.   As recently as 1893-94 other improvements were effected.
A new west window was given by the present rector (the Rev. F. Paynter) in
memory of the Rev. S. Paynter ; the old belfry was done away with, and a
new one provided in the tower on the floor above, and a portion of the gallery
cut away.   The organ was removed from this gallery to the chancel end.

In the history of the benefice one episode specially calls for notice.
Originally in the possession of the King, the advowson passed to the Prior of
Lewes, reverting thence to the Crown at the dissolution of the monasteries ;
and ultimately, in 1549, was bought by Lawrence Stoughton.   By the latter's
son it was sold to William Hammond, and by Hammond's will it was directed
that as soon as the living should become vacant it should be held by the
Master of the Grammar School.   Accordingly, the then master of the Grammar
School, John Crow, was Rector in 1595, and was succeeded by William Hill
in 1633.

But some doubts had arisen as to the validity of the bequest, and finally, in 1650, the Corporation's rights and interest in the advowson were surrendered to Nicholas Stoughton for a rent-charge of some £10 a year. Thus the close connection which at one time seemed likely to be maintained between the Free School of the town and the village church of Stoke came to an end.

The Stoughtons figure prominently in Stoke Church. They held the Manor of Stoughton, if not from the time of the Conqueror, as one member of

ST. JOHN THE EVANGELIST, STOKE.

the family would have had us believe, certainly from the reign of John to the end of the seventeenth century, when the succession ceased, the family estates were sold, and the mansion known as Stoughton Place pulled down. Lawrence Stoughton represented Guildford in Parliament in the latter years of Elizabeth, and James I. knighted him at Bagshot in 1611. His elder son, George, was knighted in 1616, and his second son, Nicholas, was M.P. for the borough under both James I. and Charles I. Memorials in the Stoughton Chapel, at the east

end of the north aisle of the church, record the virtues and doings of various
members of the family.

Other memorials of local interest are to be found in the church. A
monument by Flaxman perpetuates the memory of Mrs. Harriet Aldersey, and
a marble tablet recalls the name of Mrs. Charlotte Smith, authoress of " The
Old Manor House," and other stories which enjoyed much popularity a century
ago. A tablet in the north aisle records the death, in 1783, of Dr. James Price,
who, as " the last of the alchemists," figured prominently and discreditably in
the scientific history of his day. While practising as a physician in Guildford,
he claimed, in 1782, to have performed experiments in which he had transmuted
mercury into gold or silver. His story was, that he had placed mercury with
other ingredients containing no gold into a crucible, and had heated them; that
he had then added a red powder, and the crucible was again heated, and on
being allowed to cool had been found to contain a globule of pure gold.
Similarly by the use of a white powder, it was averred that he had produced a
globule of silver. The story was readily accepted, and Price leapt at once into
fame. He was created a Doctor of Physic by the University of Oxford, and
was elected a Fellow of the Royal Society. But the day of reckoning quickly
came. Awkward questions were asked, and Price was requested to repeat his
experiment under the eyes of a Committee of the Royal Society under pain of
expulsion. A day was appointed for the test, but Price failed to face it. Rather
than submit to inevitable disgrace, he took a draught of prussic acid, thus
dying (1783) at the early age of twenty-five. A portrait of Price, by John
Russell, R.A., is in the possession of the Guildford and Working Men's
Institute.

To meet the increasing requirements of the parish of Stoke, three additional
churches have been erected in recent years—Christ Church in Waterden Road,
within the municipal boundary; St. Saviour's, at present in a temporary building,
for which a new ecclesiastical district has been formed, also within the borough;
and Emmanuel Church at Stoughton.

A few lines must be added with reference to Stoke Hospital. This old-
fashioned red-brick building, in the Stoke Road, half-way between the Church
and the High Street, was built in 1796 for six poor and aged widows of Stoke or
Worplesdon. Its founders were William and Henry Parson, retired bakers of
Guildford, concerning whose wealth a curious story is quoted by Russell from
the *Gentleman's Magazine* for May, 1799. The parents of the two Parsons
lived at 126, High Street, now Mr. John Cable's business premises, and whilst
there found, it is said, a considerable sum of money in a vault under the cellar.
The story runs, " Mrs. Parson one evening examining whether the house was

safe, on searching the cellar fancied a part of it sounded hollow, and on calling her husband they sent the servant to bed, and, pulling up the pavement, found a complete dry arched vault. They acknowledged they thus found the vault, but were shy of speaking of anything farther. However, that they found money was little doubted, as their circumstances were from that period considerably improved." The evidence will hardly be considered convincing. But it is at any rate clear that William and Henry Parson were wealthy men, and left a considerable fortune at their death.

Any adequate notice of the history of Nonconformity in and around Guildford lies, of course, outside the scope of these pages. But a few salient facts may be cursorily mentioned. We read of " Conventicles " in Guildford and at Artington in the latter half of the seventeenth century, and the local records of the Congregationalists carry us back for over two hundred years. Originally this body worshipped in the building known as the Independent Chapel in Chapel Street—formerly Black Horse Lane. Their fortunes varied from time to time, despite the fact that one retired clergyman left them an endowment, now of considerable value, and shared with the Congregationalists at Dorking. In 1802, however, the old building was pulled down, and a fairly capacious brick chapel erected. In 1861 the late Rev. John Hart accepted the pastorate, and the effects of his energetic and courageous ministry were apparent in the removal from Chapel Street to North Street, which speedily followed. The new chapel in this thoroughfare was opened on September 24, 1863, and twenty years later a spacious Sunday-school and lecture hall was provided on an adjacent site. The buildings stand to-day as memorials of a vigour and earnestness of purpose on Mr. Hart's part which Guildford Non-conformists must always have in grateful remembrance.

Much of the same zeal has been shown of late by the Wesleyans, under the Rev. J. Telford, in the erection of a new chapel in North Street, in lieu of the edifice built on the same spot in 1843.

14

CHAPTER X.

FEW fragments of old Guildford are still visible in Milmead, when the river is crossed by the town mills on the way to St. Catherine's. But one curious relic of the past, although it survived its use for a good many years, has long since disappeared. The "ducking-stool" once stood in the Mill Pool below the old bridge. How or when this "terror for scolds and unquiet women" came to be established in the town there is no evidence to show. True, a legend runs that in 1286, Swafham, Bishop of Winchester, obtained license from the Pope to erect a ducking-stool in his diocese, which he more or less veraciously declared was "so over-run with scolds that the church bells could not be heard for their tongues on a Sunday." And it may be that the permission the Bishop thus secured was taken advantage of in Guildford. But on this point the records are silent. It appears, however, from the Austen MSS., that in 1551 Jane Wryte, wife of George Wryte, of Guildford, suffered carting and ducking ; and Russell mentions, without specifying the date, that "the last time the chair was taken out for use, one Margaret —— left the town through fear, she having long been a reputed scold."

Pleasanter traditions cluster round St. Catherine's Hill. Possibly the name of "Drake Hill," which once attached to this steep sandy bank overhanging the Portsmouth Road, referred to the Grisly Worm or Fire Drake, fabulous stories of which are so often associated with similar hills. But on one point local folk-lore is very definite. We are positively assured that St. Catherine's Chapel and its twin chapel of St. Martha were built by two giant sisters, who erected the walls with their own hands, and used a mammoth hammer, which they flung from one hill to the other as it was wanted. Guildford, however, as the reader will hardly need to be reminded, can claim no monopoly of primeval giantesses of this stamp, for corresponding stories are met with in many other parts of the country.

If, then, we turn from fable to fact, we find good reason for believing that a chapel existed here in the twelfth century. We cannot say whether it was provided for the tenants of the King's manor of Ertindon, or Artington, after its severance from that of Godalming, or whether, as Mr. Ralph Nevill would have us believe, it was the church of a population on the hill, who afterwards descended and formed the town of Guildford. But we know that very early in the fourteenth century Richard de Wauncey, Rector of St. Nicolas, purchased the site in order to annex it to his benefice as a chapel of ease. De Wauncey rebuilt the edifice which then stood upon the hill, and in May, 1317, obtained a

ST. CATHERINE'S CHAPEL.

license for its consecration. From a financial standpoint this was a good stroke of business. For, owing to the position of the chapel, directly on the Pilgrims' Way, the revenues derived from the travellers to and from Canterbury were considerable. So much so, indeed, that they appear to have aroused the envy of the Rector of St. Mary's. A dispute ensued between the rectors, which extended over some years. Finally De Wauncey's successor at St. Nicolas, Bernard Brocas, won the day, and in 1329 the chapel was reconsecrated, and attached once and for all to St. Nicolas.

The chapel has long been roofless and dismantled. Even of late years little or nothing has been done to preserve it from the hands of the despoiler or the ravages of time. But, scanty as the ruins are, they are sufficient to indicate the Early Decorated character of the building, and, as Mr. Nevill has pointed out, the windows closely resemble those of the same date in the St. John the Baptist's Chapel in St. Mary's Church. The two doorways cut into the stone-work high up in the chapel long puzzled observers. Mr. Thackeray Turner, however, has put forward a theory which seems to offer a sufficiently plausible explanation. His suggestion is that the chapel contained some relic or object of special sanctity, which was visited in such large numbers by the Canterbury pilgrims that it was found expedient to enable two distinct streams of visitors to pass by the high altar—one on the ground-floor and one above. To accomplish this, two doorways were made in the walls above the level of the floor, with external staircases of wood, and a wooden gangway across the church.

As it stands to-day, St. Catherine's is undoubtedly a picturesque object in the landscape, and its broken windows form not inappropriate frames for lovely peeps across the valley of the Wey, to the clustering roofs of Guildford on the one hand, and on the other to the distant ridge of Hindhead beyond the spire of Godalming.

Apparently Richard de Wauncey had in view other possibilities of revenue besides offerings from Canterbury pilgrims. He procured a royal charter for the establishment of an annual fair at St. Catherine's for five days, at which "every inhabitant of the manor was permitted to sell ale on payment of a small acknowledgment to the lord." This fair long retained its popularity, and the charter (*vide* the Loseley MSS.) was confirmed by Henry VIII. A characteristic sketch of the scene by Turner appears in the "Liber Studiorum," bearing date 1811. A few stalls and a small crowd may still be seen at the foot of and on the slopes of the hill on October 2, and the tolls may still be claimed by the Rector of St. Nicolas if he thinks fit. But the old-time glories of the fair have of course long since departed.

If, with a glance at the picturesque manor house of Braboeuf, we quit St. Catherine's and make our way westward along Sandy Lane, Loseley soon comes within view. No mansion in the county is richer in historic interest, and none has more beautiful surroundings.

The story of Loseley has never yet been told with the skill and complete-ness with which Mr. Frederic Harrison has given us the history of Sutton Place. But abundant materials are easily at hand for the brief glance at its past which these pages permit. We need not pause to note the earlier records of the manor: it will suffice to remember that Loseley was purchased early in the sixteenth century by Sir Christopher More, and that the house, as we see it to-day, owes its chief features to his son, Sir William, by whom it was erected between 1562 and 1568. A west wing was added by Sir William's son, George,

LOSELEY.

(From a Photograph by Mr. E. M. Brownsword.)

and included a long gallery and a chapel from the designs of John Thorpe, whose scheme contemplated the addition of a corresponding wing on the east side, with a wall and central gatehouse on the north side, to complete the quadrangle. But this wing was allowed to get into a very ruinous condition, and was taken down about seventy years ago. Despite this loss, the house as it stands to-day, with its gray stone gables, its mullioned windows, and its wainscoted walls, is an exceptionally interesting and valuable specimen of the domestic architecture of its period. It is now owned by Mr. W. More-Molyneux, a descendant of Sir Thomas Molyneux (died 1710), whose wife, Margaret More,

LOSELEY CHAPEL, OR, ST. NICHOLAS CHURCH.

was the sole inheritrix of the Loseley estate. Both by Mr. Molyneux and his father much has been done to preserve, and, in the best sense of the word, to restore, the old mansion.

The two chief apartments are the great hall and the drawing room. The former contains portraits of Edward VI. (Holbein), James I., and Anne of Denmark (Mytens), and a number of family portraits. Some curious paintings on canvas of the arms and badges of the Tudor kings, let into the oak panelling on the walls, are believed to have been brought from Nonsuch Palace when it was pulled down about the year 1700. The drawing-room is specially noteworthy for the elaborate chimney-piece executed in native chalk, the carved ceiling, the rich cornice with the rebus of the More family—a mulberry-tree intersecting the motto, "Morus tarde moriens. Morum cito moriturum" and the portraits of Anne Boleyn, Sir William and Sir George More, and other members of the family. There is also a portrait of Thomas More, the Chancellor, who, however, was of a different family from the Mores of Loseley. There are two low gilt chairs in this room for which Queen Elizabeth is said to have worked some cushions. Loseley and its owners stood so high in the Queen's estimation that she thrice visited the mansion. The grounds are not less interesting than the house itself. The broad grass terrace, which overlooks the partly filled-in moat, the yew hedges, the old-fashioned flowers in the borders, and the quaint pigeon-house at each corner of the wall—these are all in perfect keeping with the stately mansion, and help to carry us back in thought to the days when the Virgin Queen herself may have paced the close, smooth-shaven turf.

The historic associations of the spot are, indeed, in some respects unique. It is scarcely possible to name a private mansion in the country which can boast of greater treasures than have been found in the muniment-room of Loseley. Centuries ago it became the depository of documents now of priceless value to the antiquary and historian, and it is interesting to trace the series of events which led to this accumulation of literary material beneath a single roof.

First and foremost we owe the Loseley MSS. to Sir William More. Born 1519-20, Sir William was "a man of affairs from his early manhood to his late decay." A Justice of the Peace for the county of Surrey, he was "remarkable throughout Elizabeth's reign for the zeal and pleasure he exhibited in transacting the public business of his division of the Shire." Further, he was a Deputy-Lieutenant, and twice held the office of Sheriff; he represented Guildford in several Parliaments, and was subsequently elected Knight of his native shire. Above all, he stood high in Elizabeth's favour, and during a great part of her reign was her agent in matters of state in every hundred of Surrey. Other circumstances, however, contributed to the value and variety of the historical documents Sir William preserved. He was the friend, and ultimately the executor, of Sir Thomas Cawarden, a London citizen, who was Keeper of the Tents, Master of the Revels, during the reigns of Henry VIII., Edward VI. and Mary, and Keeper of the Palace and Parks of Nonsuch under Henry VIII. As Master of the Revels Cawarden was a supreme theatrical manager before the establishment of permanent public theatres, and the official correspondence carried on by and with him in this capacity is of vital importance in its bearing on one section of our literary history. On Cawarden's death these writings passed to Sir William More, and thus helped to enrich the archives of Loseley.

THE STUDIO OF MR. G. F. WATTS, R.A. AT LIMNERSLEASE, COMPTON.

15

Not less helpful to the same result was the prominence in the public life of his time which was gained by Sir William's son and successor. Sir George More indeed rivalled, if he did not eclipse, his father in the extent and importance of his official work. He represented Guildford and Surrey in successive Parliaments, and was a familiar figure in the Courts of Elizabeth and James, and Receiver-General and Treasurer to Henry, Prince of Wales, Chancellor of the Order of the Garter, and Lieutenant of the Tower during the imprisonment of the Earl and Countess of Somerset. Much of his official correspondence is to be found among the multifarious records of Loseley.

Again, Sir William More's sister Elizabeth had for her third husband Lord Keeper Egerton, afterwards Lord Chancellor Ellesmere, and the letters addressed by the Chancellor to his father-in-law and his brother-in-law also form a valuable section of the domestic correspondence preserved in this Surrey mansion.

An unfounded story at one time gained currency, that the key of the Loseley muniment-room was lost for over 200 years. Mr. A. J. Kempe's volume, published 1835, on the Loseley MSS., and various contributions to the "Archaeologia," sufficed only to indicate a small portion of the mass of materials accessible to the student. And the truth was not fully told until Mr. J. Cordy Jeaffreson presented his exhaustive report to the Royal Commission on Historical MSS. In all, Mr Jeaffreson catalogued 2,240 MSS., of which no less than 1,447 relate to the "spacious times of great Elizabeth."

Slightly to the west of Loseley lies the village of Compton, noteworthy for its church. We need not concern ourselves with the disputable statement that much of this quaint village church dates from the time of the Domesday Survey. Apparently no part of the building is earlier than the middle of the twelfth century,[*] and although some good Norman, Transitional Norman, and Early English work may well receive attention, the distinctive and remarkable feature of the building is the fact that it possesses (1) a two-storied chancel, and (2), perhaps the oldest piece of Norman woodwork known in England.

The double chancel – or, rather, double sanctuary, for the upper story extends only over the sanctuary bay – is, indeed, considered unique in this country. A beautifully enriched Norman arch separates the chancel from the nave. A few feet east of this arch the chancel is again crossed by a low semi-circular arch, which supports a floor forming the roof or ceiling of the sanctuary bay below, and also thus providing the second or upper story. Originally this upper sanctuary may possibly have been reached from the exterior of the church by a separate staircase, for which a doorway, now blocked up, seems to

[*] Mr. Lewis André, in "Surrey Archæological Society's Collections,' vol. xii., part ii.

have been provided. At the present time it is approached by wooden stairs within the church.

The wooden screen which fences in the front of this upper chapel is, as I have said, the oldest known example of woodwork in the country. Its date is thought to be 1180, and it exhibits the "earliest form in which wooden screen-work appeared in the Gothic style." It comprises nine round-headed arches, carried on octagonal pillars, which spring from a solid beam or cellar, capped by a massive cornice.

Compton, in many respects a typical Surrey village, boasts one distinguished resident whose name is honoured wherever English art is known. Not far from the village Mr. G. F. Watts, R.A., has found in Limnerslease a sequestered and picturesque country home.

THE STAIRCASE, LEVYL'S DENE, MERROW.
(From a contemporary drawing by Mr. W. S. Archer.)

CHAPTER XI.

PORT in one form or another has held sway upon Merrow Downs for a century or more. These breezy uplands were long the scene of the Guildford Races, formerly held at Whitsuntide, and for many years largely patronized. The meeting, moreover, enjoyed royal patronage, for one of the chief items in the programme was the King's purse of a hundred guineas, originally given by William III., and continued by succeeding monarchs. Eclipse, ever famous in the history of the turf, walked over for this event in 1770. Early in this century, however, the popularity of the fixture began to wane, partly, it is said, from an inconvenient alteration in the date of the meeting, and partly from the absence of any influential patrons of the sport in the immediate neighbourhood. Ultimately the fixture was abandoned after the races of 1854. Golf now flourishes on the Downs, and the Guildford Golf Club—one of the earliest formed, as well as one of the most prosperous clubs in the home counties— has been fortunate enough to secure on these invigorating slopes links which justly rank high in the favour of votaries of the game, and a Club-house which commands lovely views.

The prospect from the Downs is indeed varied and extensive. One noticeable feature in the scene is the picturesque ivy-clad house known as Levyl's Dene, nestling among the trees which hide from view the Epsom Road as it wends its way to Merrow Church. Levyl's Dene is, in fact, the oldest house in Merrow parish. It was for a time the huntsman's house, was afterwards occupied as the dower-house by Mrs. Onslow, mother of the present Earl of Onslow, until her death, and is now the residence of Sir Charles Stuart Rich, Bart. Externally the house has in some respects suffered severely before passing into the hands of the present owner. The modern addition on the west side was a particularly unfortunate erection.   An avenue, a fine triple one, formerly ran from the house right across the Downs, but was cut down by the late Earl of Onslow. But, despite these losses, Levyl's Dene still merits attention.   The remarkable thickness of the ivy is in itself proof of the age of the older portion of the building ; and internally the hall, with the fine staircase of curious design, the dining-room and the drawing-room—the latter used as a storeroom during the reign of the huntsman—with their extremely good oak panelling and the exquisitely carved chimney-places, combine to make the house, though small, distinctly picturesque and interesting.

Merrow Church, which lies a little further eastward, also at the foot of the

LEVYL'S DENE, MERROW.

Downs, was almost entirely rebuilt in 1843-44, but the old Norman arches and doorways were retained.   In 1872 a south chancel aisle, which was the burial-place of the Onslow family for nearly a couple of centuries, and contains the grave of Speaker Onslow, was restored by the present Earl.   The bodies were removed from the aisle and placed in the family vault in the churchyard.

When the pedestrian makes his way from the Merrow Downs through " Fairyland " to Newlands Corner, he is well repaid by the magnificent prospect afforded at this well-known spot, famous also for the old yew-trees which still

MIDDLESEX HALL AND ANNEX, WOMEN.

flourish in the chalky soil near at hand. On the right the Chantry Woods lead
up to the sandy hill which is crowned by the lonely chapel of St. Martha's.
Below are the grand old trees and leafy slopes of Albury Park, with the
crocketed tower of the Irvingite Church a conspicuous object in the landscape ;
whilst further eastward along the valley lies the village of Shere, although
almost wholly hidden from sight. But the eye can range much further afield
than this—south to the high range of hills which overlook the weald of Sussex ;
south-west to the distant ridges of Hindhead and Blackdown ; south-east to the
tower-capped Leith Hill ; and northward over the comparatively level country
which stretches away beyond St. George's Hills to the smoke-canopied Metropolis.
One writer has aptly declared that the whole scene recalls some wide-sweeping
landscape by Rubens or Turner. Not less apt or true were the words of the
late Louis Jennings, when he wrote of this spot, " It tempts one to linger over
it, to sit down and enjoy it, slowly and peacefully, and make a feast of it."

The road to Shere passes close by the deep glen in which is situated the
Silent Pool. The romantic tale traditionally associated with this spot is well
known, and formed the groundwork of Martin Tupper's story of " Stephan
Langton." King John, so the legend runs, became enamoured of the fair
daughter of a woodman living here. The girl was surprised by him whilst she
was bathing in the pool, and in her terror releasing her hold of a branch of a
tree, she sank with a loud scream into deep water. Her brother, a goat-herd,
rushed to her aid when he heard her cry for help, and plunged into the pool.
But, unable to save her, he shared his sister's fate. For generations after, the
legend continues, the figure of a girl with her arms clasped round her brother
might be seen at midnight beneath the still and silent surface of the pool.

Shere, known at different periods of its history as " Essira " " Schyre,"
" Schire," " Shyre," " Sheire," " Shire," and " Shere," well deserves its reputation
as one of the most charming villages in this lovely district. Beauty abounds at
every turn. Deeply-wooded lanes almost Devonian in their character, Downs
bright with heather bordering and protecting the valley, picturesque water-mills,
quaint old cottages and houses—these are some of the characteristics which have
won for Shere the favour and the affection both of artists and literary men.
Grote, the historian, had his country residence here, and Mrs. Grote is buried in
the village churchyard. To-day Mr. B. W. Leader is the most gifted member
of the numerous band of painters who find inspiration for brush and pencil in and
around the vale. Above all, Shere is linked with the Bray family, whose
intimate connections with local history extend back for five centuries or more.
Sir R. Bray, as we have already seen, was custodian of the royal park and
manor in Guildford in Henry VII.'s time, and was a liberal benefactor to the

16

Dominican Friars in the town. To William Bray, the editor of Evelyn's "Diary," we in more modern days owe, jointly with Manning, almost the first history of the county worthy of the name. At the present time Mr. Reginald More Bray occupies an official position as Recorder of Guildford, which at least serves to mark these old local associations. Several monuments of the Bray family are to be seen in Shere Church, and noticeable among the remains of the old glass is the bray, or hemp-breaker, the device of Sir Reginald Bray. The church itself is a somewhat quaint mixture of styles. The south door is Norman, the rest of the building is chiefly Decorated, and a small chapel projects from the church on the north side, forming, with heavy buttresses, a strong if cumbersome support to the tower.

Albury Park, now the property of the Duke of Northumberland, by his marriage with the eldest daughter of the late Mr. Henry Drummond, M.P., lies on our left, if we return towards Guildford by the valley road. Here two churches claim attention. After the estate had passed into the possession of Mr. Drummond in 1826, the old parish church, situated in the park, and within a stone's-throw of the house, was discarded and dismantled, and a new church built much nearer to the village. But the earlier fabric still stands, perhaps the oldest church in the county. Portions of the tower are thought to have every appearance of Saxon work, and it has been suggested that the bases of the columns of the nave were brought from a temple belonging to the Roman settlement which undoubtedly existed close by on Farley Heath. The chapel at the end of the south aisle, richly decorated by Pugin, is set apart as a mortuary chapel for the Drummond family, and Mr. Henry Drummond himself is buried there. To Mr. Drummond is also due the erection on the confines of the park of the church, or "cathedral," in which the local community of the Catholic Apostolic Church worship. It is Perpendicular in style, and the internal decorations are rich and effective.

The gardens of Albury Park, however, have more often won praise than its churches. Cobbett's eulogy of them has been frequently quoted. They were, he thought, the prettiest he ever beheld, and showed taste and judgment at every step. They owe their main features to John Evelyn, who in 1667, at the request of the then Earl of Arundel, was responsible for the design. In some respects Evelyn's work has since been modified; the canal, for example, has been drained. But for the fine terrace under the hill a quarter of a mile long, "of the finest greensward, and as level as a die," and the famous yew-hedge, equally long, ten feet high, and perhaps the finest in the country, Albury has still to thank John Evelyn.

Immediately above us, as we journey still further westward along the valley, is St. Martha's Hill, capped by the chapel which is so conspicuous and familiar a landmark for many miles around. We know relatively little of the history which must attach to such a spot. The very name—for the church was once dedicated to all Holy Martyrs—opens up suggestions of a past rich in interest. But the actual records are slight. Of the original founder we have no trace, although some fragments of Norman work were to be detected in the ruins

TREES IN ALBURY PARK.
(From a photograph by Mr. F. M. Brownrigg)

which long remained as the uncared-for vestiges of the early fabric. We know that the chapel was attached to the manor of Chilworth, which was held by Bishop Odo of Bayeux under the Conqueror, and that from its position on the Pilgrims' Way it grew rapidly in importance in the twelfth and thirteenth centuries. A new chancel was built in 1186, and dedicated to St. Thomas à Becket. Later on the manor of Chilworth, with the chapel, was given by Edward III. to the priory of Newark, and there is reason for believing that the old house at the foot of the hill, known as Tyting Farm (in which an ancient oratory has been discovered), was the dwelling-place of the priest in charge of St. Martha's. A century or two afterwards the chapel fell into decay. In 1463 forty days' indulgence were granted by Bishop William of Wayntlete to all pilgrims resorting to the shrine who should contribute to its maintenance or repair, or there repeat a Pater Noster, an Ave, and the Apostles' Creed. But these efforts availed little, and after the dissolution of the monasteries St. Martha's was allowed year by year to lapse into ruin till 1848, when it was virtually rebuilt and restored for worship.

One local tradition which Mr. Martin Tupper also utilized in his " Stephan Langton " has been the subject of some recent controversy. The legend is that Langton, while a monk at Newark, was one of the priests in charge of St. Martha's who resided at Tyting House, and that his desire was to be buried in the sanctuary near the altar where he first ministered, and near the body of " the fair Alice," whom he had dearly loved long before he had taken the celibate's vow. We are told that his wish was duly respected, and that St. Martha's was actually his last resting-place, while the monks of Canterbury buried in state an empty coffin. In the spring of 1890, however, discoveries at Canterbury threw some doubt upon this romantic tradition. Father Morris, after carefully examining some remains which had been exposed to view in the cathedral, pronounced them to be those of Langton. But this conclusion was stoutly challenged in more quarters than one, and the discussion which ensued leaves matters perhaps scarcely more satisfactorily determined than they were before. In whatever direction the balance of probability may lie, it is certain that the old Surrey story will not willingly be allowed to die by those to whom the lonely chapel on the hilltop appeals as a familiar if silent friend.

From St. Martha's we overlook Blackheath, the scene of a volunteer review in 1864, and where recent erections include a uniquely-decorated mission chapel, dedicated to St. Martin, and an important Roman Catholic monastery. A little to the west is Great Tangley, with its fine half-timbered manor house, bearing date 1582, and long used as a farmhouse, but most judiciously repaired and added to by Mr. Wickham Flower.

Rich and varied as is the view from St. Martha's, it scarcely equals that from Newlands Corner. Yet, as one glances at the lovely vale of Chilworth at one's feet, the words of Cobbett - so often quoted, it must again be said - inevitably recur. We can smile, of course, at his violent rhetoric condemning the powder-works originally established by Evelyn, of Long Ditton, in Elizabethan days and the paper-mills for the manufacture of bank-notes, as " two of the most damnable inventions that every sprang from the mind of man under the influence of the Devil." But we can join in his eulogy of "this tranquil spot, where the nightingales are to be heard earlier and later than in any other part of England, where the first bursting of the buds is seen in spring ;" and we can agree with him in thinking that the valley " seems to have been created by a bountiful Providence as one of the choicest retreats of man."

Shalford, part of which is so rapidly becoming virtually a suburb of Guildford, must have owed much in the old days to the Canterbury pilgrims.

Its fair in August rivalled, if it did not eclipse, in importance that of St. Catherine's. So large was the attendance, in fact, that the churchyard, the original venue, had to be forsaken for greater accommodation in the fields by the riverside, where, it is said, no less than 150 acres of ground were at one time utilized for the purposes of the fair.   To-day Shalford boasts of a characteristic Surrey green, and a prettily-designed modern church, near which the remnants of the stocks may still be noticed.   The church, built 1846, stands on the site of a fabric mentioned in Domesday, and is the fourth of which we have record. The manor house close by can make little claim to architectural distinction ; but, as has already been noted, there is reason for thinking that some of the materials obtained by George Austen in 1608, upon the demolition of the Guildford Friary, were utilized in the house then erected on this site for the family. The present mansion contains a fine carved oak chimney-piece preserved from the Elizabethan house, and, as the property of Lieutenant-Colonel Godwin Austen, it is linked with the history of Guildford by many honourable associations.

Mr. Frederic Harrison, as I have already remarked, has once for all told the story of Sutton Place and the Westons. Space must, nevertheless, be found

SHALFORD OLD CHURCH, BUILT 1789, PULLED DOWN 1843.
(From a print in the possession of Lord Ashcombe.)

for a few facts culled from the information he has thus placed within reach. Sutton owes its existence to Sir Richard Weston, "one of those able and devoted servants of Henry VIII, who built up the elaborate fabric of adminis- tration and created the centralized power of the Tudor dynasty." Born about 1465, and dying in 1541, he was throughout his long life in the closest personal relations with Henry. He remained attached to the King's household alike under the Reformed and the Catholic faith, alike under Cromwell and Wolsey, and under the first four wives of Henry VIII. Even the tragedy which befell his son Francis, who was beheaded on Tower Hill as one of Ann Boleyn's lovers, seems, says Mr. Harrison, to have made no difference in the position of the father. "Sir Richard retained his offices and the confidence of the King; he lived six years after at Sutton, which was the King's gift. And his widow, when the royal family are at Guildford, sends presents of pudding, peacocks, herons, and 'sweet bagges.'"

In the seventeenth century Sutton was occupied by the founder's great-grandson, Sir Richard, who promoted the canalisation of the Wey, and introduced from Flanders the contrivance of locks and flood-gates.

As for the house itself, there is reason to think that it was built about 1523-1525. Brick and terra-cotta were the materials employed, no stone

SHALFORD CHURCH, 1895.
(From a photograph by Mr. A. L. Mesn.)

whatever being used in the construction or ornamentation. It is, says Mr. Harrison, the unique work of some unknown master, "one of the landmarks in the history of English architecture, and one of the earliest existing specimens of the purely domestic mansion-house entirely planned and constructed in an era when no purpose of defence was thought of, and when modern ideas of domestic economy had fully developed. . . . It is so far modern that it has all the symmetry of a Paladian design, whilst it has no single classical feature, such as occur at every point of a building of Renaissance times. It is interesting to speculate what might have been the future of English domestic architecture if it had sought to adapt and retain the Gothic forms to new uses in the refined and graceful spirit of the builder of Sutton."

Originally the house formed a quadrangle, but the side which contained the entrance gateway was removed toward the end of last century. Within, much alteration has been made, but many of the older fittings still remain, and Sutton, now the property of Mr. Salvin, is undoubtedly entitled to high place among the unique features of interest in the countryside within easy reach of the old county town.

THE DRAWING-ROOM, LEVYE'S DENE, MERROW.

GUILDFORD MEMORANDA.

MEMBERS OF PARLIAMENT FOR GUILDFORD SINCE 1800.

1802 Hon. Thomas Onslow (afterwards Viscount Cranley).
General the Hon. Chapp'e Norton (brother of Lord Grantley).
1806 Hon. Thomas Onslow, re-elected.
George Holme Sumner, elected by a majority of two over General Norton, who was afterwards reseated by a Committee of the House of Commons.
1807 General Norton.
Colonel the Hon. T. Cranley Onslow second son of the 2nd Earl).
1812 Colonel the Hon. T. C. Onslow.
Arthur Onslow (Serjeant-at-Law), of Send Grove.
1818 Mr. Serjeant Onslow.
Mr. Serjeant Best (afterwards Lord Wynford).
1819 Mr. Serjeant Best being appointed a Welsh Judge, Mr. Charles Baring Wall was elected.
1820 Mr. Serjeant Onslow } re-elected.
Charles Baring Wall {
1826 Mr. Serjeant Onslow.
Hon. G. Chapple Norton (brother of Lord Grantley).
1830 George Holme Sumner.
Charles Baring Wall.
1831 James Mangles.
Hon. Charles Francis Norton
1832 James Mangles.
Charles Baring Wall.
1835 James Mangles.
Charles Baring Wall.
1837 Charles Baring Wall.

1837 Hon. J. Yorke Scarlett (second son of Lord Abinger).
1841 Ross Donelly Mangles.
Charles Baring Wall.
1837 Henry Currie.
Ross Donelly Mangles.
1852 Ross Donelly Mangles.
James Bell.
1857 William Bovill.
Guildford Onslow.
1859 William Bovill.
Guildford Onslow.
1862 Guildford Onslow.
William Bovill.
1865 Guildford Onslow.
Sir William Bovill.
1866 Richard Garth (in the place of Sir W. Bovill, promoted to the Judicial Bench).
By the Act of 1868 the borough was deprived of one member.
1868 Guildford Onslow.
1874 Denzil Robert Onslow.
1880 Denzil Robert Onslow.
By the Redistribution Act of 1885 the borough of Guildford was disfranchised, and one member was assigned to the South-West (or Guildford) Division of Surrey. The elections since this change have resulted as follows :
1885 Hon. W. St. John Brodrick. 4,485.
Mr. E. D. Gosling, 3,730.
1886 Hon. W. St. John Brodrick, unopposed.
1892 Hon. W. St. John Brodrick, 5,191.
Mr. George Lawrence, 3,720.

MAYORS OF GUILDFORD SINCE 1800.

1800 John Nealds.
1800 Richard Sparkes.
1801 John Nealds.
1802 John Martyr.
1803 James Vincent.
1804 Robert Harrison.
1805 Samuel Russell.
1806 George Waugh.
1807 Charles Booker.

1808 John Nealds.
1809 John Martyr.
1810 John French.
1811 Joseph Hockley.
1812 John Tickner.
1813 John Nealds.
1814 Charles Booker.
1815 George Waugh.
1816 William Elkins.

1817 John Martyr.
1818 Joseph Haydon.
1819 John Nealds.
1820 John Nealds.
1821 William Sparkes.
1822 John French.
1823 Charles Booker.
1824 William Elkins.
1825 James Stedman.
1826 William Sparkes.
1827 John Rand.
1828 George Waugh.
1829 Joseph Haydon.
1830 William Elkins.
1831 Charles Booker.
1832 James Stedman.
1833 William Sparkes.
1834 John Rand.
1835 John Rand.
1836 (On January 1, after the passing of the Municipal Corporation Act) John Small-peice.
1836 (On November 9) Anthony Lee.
1837 Joseph Haydon.
1838 William Sparkes.
1839 James Stedman.
1840 Joseph Haydon.
1841 William Edmund Elkins.
1842 Joseph Weale.
1843 Cassteels Cooper.
1844 William King.
1845 Joseph Haydon.
1846 Thomas Jenner Sells.
1847 Joseph Weale.
1848 Joseph Weale.
1849 John Ryde Cooke.
1850 Samuel Haydon.
1851 Thomas Jenner Sells.
1852 William Taylor.
1853 Joseph Weale.
1854 John Ryde Cooke.

1855 William Edmund Elkins.
1856 Samuel Haydon.
1857 William Edmund Elkins.
1858 Henry Piper.
1859 Henry Piper.
1860 John Palmer.
1861 William Edmund Elkins.
1862 Henry Piper.
1863 Philip Whittington Jacob.
1864 Philip Whittington Jacob.
1865 Philip Whittington Jacob.
1866 Philip Whittington Jacob.
1867 Edward Thomas Upperton.
1868 Edward Thomas Upperton.
1869 Dodsworth Haydon.
1870 Edward Thomas Upperton.
1871 Hoffgaard Shoobridge.
1872 William Triggs.
1873 William Triggs.
1874 Edward Thomas Upperton.
1875 Philip William Lovell.
1876 William Triggs.
1877 Frederick Augustine Crooke.
1878 Frederick Thomas Lethbridge.
1879 Frederick Thomas Lethbridge.
1880 Edward Thomas Upperton.
1881 William Triggs.
1882 William Triggs.
1883 Edward Thomas Upperton.
1884 John Mason.
1885 John Mason.
1886 William Swayne (Her Majesty's Jubilee).
1887 William Swayne.
1888 Thomas Stephenson.
1889 Thomas Stephenson.
1890 William Wells.
1891 William Wells.
1892 William Swayne.
1893 George Tayler.
1894 Robert Salsbury.

RECORDERS.

The office of Recorder has been filled as follows during the past century :

	APPOINTED.		APPOINTED.
William, Lord Grantley	1789.	Hon. George Chapple Norton	1823.
Mr. Serjeant Draper Best (afterwards Lord Wynford)	1808.	His Honour Morgan Howard. Q.C.	1875.
Mr. Serjeant Onslow	1819.	Mr. Reginald More Bray	May, 1891.

HIGH STEWARDS.

	APPOINTED.		APPOINTED.
George, Earl of Onslow	1776.	Fletcher Grantley	1835.
William, Lord Grantley	1814.	William Hillier, Earl of Onslow	October, 1875.

NOTE. Mr. Edwin Bonner has kindly supplied much of the information in the above tables.

RECORD OF MUNICIPAL ELECTIONS.

The following figures give the pollings during the last twenty-one years.

1874.
Jefiries ... 535
Haydon ... 493
White ... 491
Nye ... 484
Holt ... 394
Smith ... 378
Mason ... 372

1875.
Stevens ... 504
Williamson, W. ... 487
Colebrook ... 455
Jeffery ... 453
Swayne ... 443
Bullen ... 436
Boting ... 386
Pigott ... 352

1876.
Swayne ... 589
Boxall ... 546
Lovett ... 527
Lethbridge ... 509
Bullen ... 498
Billing, J. ... 468
Hitchcook ... 454
Stephenson ... 413

1877.
Haydon ... 617
Bullen ... 570
Drewett ... 548
Nye ... 537
Moon ... 507
White ... 467
Hitchcook ... 444
Jeffries ... 422

1878.
Stevens ... 616
Hitchcock ... 602
Williamson, W. ... 538
Colebrook ... 528
Mason ... 525
Smith ... 501
Jacobs ... 417

1879.
Lethbridge ... 775
White ... 737
Mason, J. ... 721
Withers ... 642
Boxall ... 633
Swayne ... 598
Stephenson ... 597
Bull ... 551

1880.
Haydon ... 634
Boxall ... 630
Bullen ... 609
Wells ... 573
Nye ... 571
Stephenson ... 503
Pimm ... 544
Jeffries ... 446

1881.
Hitchcock ... 750
Stevens ... 727
Swayne ... 664
Bowyer ... 645
Asher ... 644
Colebrook ... 567
Lydgate ... 553
Williamson ... 510

1882.
Mason, J. ... 710
Lethbridge ... 625
Withers ... 602
Williamson ... 600
Boting ... 515
Evans ... 419

1883.
Holden ... 818
Bullen ... 751
Colebrook ... 688
Wrist ... 682
Boxall ... 647
Ashe ... 642
Leake ... 615
Wells ... 389

1884.
Hitchcock ... 842
Swayne ... 773
Boxall ... 762
Cable ... 742
Bowyer ... 736
Carling ... 733
White ... 709
Briggs ... 682

1885.
Mason, J. ... 899
Tickner ... 790
Lethbridge ... 789
Walbrook ... 779
Billing ... 765
Withers ... 729
Williamson ... 682

1886.
Holden ... 854
Bullen ... 790
Wrist ... 789
Colebrook ... 779
Dixon ... 765
Loe ... 729
Loe ... 654
Shillingford ... 659

1887.
Hitchcock ... 944
Cable ... 881
Swayne ... 742
Boxall ... 646
Boting ... 482

1888.
Tayler ... 904
Allen ... 882
Loe ... 845
Wheeler ... 832
Fulk ... 831
Briggs ... 780
Wells ... 772
Boting ... 720

1889.
Mason, J. ... 904
Bullen ... 882
Mason, R. ... 845
Briggs ... 832
Wrist ... 831
Colebrook ... 780
Fulk ... 772
Beckham ... 720

1890.
Swayne ... 1123
Cable ... 991
Wrist ... 969
Wells ... 921
Colebrook ... 908
Boxall ... 900
Rees ... 857
French ... 855

1891.
Salsbury ... 993
Wheeler ... 686
Tayler ... 951
Loe ... 917
Best ... 900
McWharrie ... 854
Rees ... 818
Bentley ... 764

1892.
Peak ... 1030
Mason, R. ... 969
Hitchcock ... 939
Briggs ... 919
Carling ... 887
Best ... 852
Allen ... 819
Martin ... 730

1893.
Bullen ... 1078
Emery ... 1024
Wells ... 1010
Wrist ... 966
Cable ... 953
Funnifield ... 928
McWharrie ... 912
Colebrook ... 822
Nash ...
Boting ...

1894.
Miles ... 1097
Tayler ... 970
Smith ... 933
Salsbury ... 926
Loe ... 838
Wheeler ... 827
Martin ... 802
Tanner ... 621

PUBLIC BUILDINGS.

The following are some of the chief public buildings erected since the publication of the last edition of Russell's " History," 1845. with the date of erection :

Stoke Parochial Schools. 1856.
S. Nicolas Infant School. 1860.
County and Borough Halls, 1862.
Congregational Chapel, 1863.
Royal Surrey County Hospital, 1866.
Fire-Engine House. 1872.
Ward Street Temperance Hall. 1876.
Congregational Sunday Schools and Lecture Hall. 1883.
Isolation Hospital, 1886.

Post-Office, North Street, 1886.
Public Baths, 1889.
Club-house of the Guildford Golf Club. Merrow Downs. 1891.
Drill Hall. 1891.
Borough Police Station. 1892.
High School for Girls, London Road, 1893.
Wesleyan Chapel, 1894.
The Guildford Sports Ground, Woodbridge Road, was opened in 1894.

MISCELLANEOUS.

THE BOROUGH BOUNDARIES. — Originally the borough consisted of the parishes of Holy Trinity and St Mary, and a portion of S. Nicolas. These were confirmed and sworn to on May 25, 1741, and they are minutely described in Russell's " History," 1801 edition, p. 175*. In 1832 the borough limits were much extended by the Reform Act, and a further extension took place in 1887.

GUILDFORD UNION comprises the following parishes : Holy Trinity. St. Mary, and S. Nicolas (Guildford ; Albury, Artington, Clandon (East), Clandon (West), Compton, Godalming, Horsley East . Horsley (West), Merrow, Ockham, Pirbright, Puttenham, Send and Ripley, Shere. Stoke, Wanborough, Wisley, and Worplesdon. The Board of Guardians first met in 1836, with the late Earl of Lovelace, then Lord King, as chairman, and Mr. James Mangles, formerly M.P. for Guildford, as vice-chairman.

RAILWAYS. In 1844 a company was formed to establish a connection with the South-Western Railway at Woking, and the line was opened on May 5, 1845. The line was extended to Portsmouth in 1859.

The " New Line " *via* Cobham and Surbiton, and *via* Effingham and Leatherhead, with a station in London Road, was opened in 1885.

The South-Eastern line from Redhill to Reading through Guildford was opened in 1849.

The London, Brighton, and South Coast Company's branch line from Horsham to Guildford was opened on October 2, 1865.

The Guildford Junction station was rebuilt in its present form in 1884.

THE OLD BRIDGE was originally built of stone, and consisted of four arches. It was closed by a bar, which was opened only when floods took place ; but when the river was canalized to Godalming, the centre arch was widened with brickwork. In 1825 a further widening was carried out.

THE NEW BRIDGE was opened on July 12, 1882.

GAS.—The Guildford Gas and Coke Company was formed in 1824, and the town was first lighted with gas on May 4 of that year.

THE WATERWORKS were purchased by the Corporation in 1864 for £9,100.

THE GUILDFORD SCHOOL BOARD was formed on April 2, 1883, the first chairman being Mr. David Williamson, J.P. Spacious schools were erected in Sydenham Road, and were enlarged in 1891.

GUILDFORD THEATRE was erected at the beginning of the century in Market Street, and Mrs. Jordan, Kean. Macready, and T. P. Cooke are among the distinguished performers who were at different times seen upon its boards. The site is now occupied by workshops belonging to Messrs. Williamson and Sons.

GUILDFORD GAOL, completed in 1822, was situated on Castle Hill, a short distance south of the castle ruins, and was utilized till the erection of the County Prison at Wandsworth in 1851, when the buildings in Guildford were disposed of.

THE GUILDFORD MECHANICS' INSTITUTION was founded in 1834, and the Guildford Literary and Scientific Institution in the following year. They were united in 1843 as the Guildford Institute. In 1856 Guildford Working Men's Institute was started. and in 1892 an amalgamation of these two organizations was effected, under the title of the Guildford and Working Men's Institution.

A MAIN DRAINAGE SCHEME for the borough, from plans designed by Mr. C. Nicholson Lailey, was adopted in 1890 ; work was begun in 1892, and the sewers were completed—although they had not been formally taken over by the Corporation at the beginning of 1895.

GUILDFORD CEMETERY, on the old Farnham Road, was consecrated in 1856.

The population of the borough in 1891 was 14,316.

INDEX.

LIST OF SUBSCRIBERS.

Aitken, Mr. T.
Arbuthnot, Mr. F. F.
Ashcombe, Right Hon. Lord (2)
Asher, Mr. A. P.
Ashford, Mr. J. B.
Ashpitel, Rev. F.
Austen, Prof. Roberts-, C.B., F.R.S.
Badcock, Mr. R. S.
Baker, Mr. James
Baker, Mr. W., J.P.
Barfoot, Mr. E. S.
Bartlett, Mr. J. (2)
Baxter, Mr. George (2)
Bean, Miss
Beck, Mr. C.
Beckham, Mr. D. C. (2)
Bell, Mrs.
Bentley, Mr. J. W.
Berry, Mr. W.
Billing, Mr. J. H.
Billing, Mr. R. T.
Billing, Mr. S.
Blaine, Mrs. (2)
Bode, Rev. J. E.
Bond, Mrs.
Bonner, Mr. E.
Bowles, Mr. A. H.
Boxall, Mrs. Jane
Brass, Mrs. J. (2)
Broughton, Miss L. D.
Brown, Mr. H.
Brownrigg, Mr. T. M.
Budgett, Mr. J. S.
Bull, Mr. A.
Burbidge, Mr. W. H.
Burgess, Mr. C.
Burrows, Rev. L. Francis
Butler, Mrs. T. M.
Cable, Mr. J.
Cable, Mr. J., J.P.
Cancellor and Hill, Messrs.
Capp, Mr. J. J.
Carbutt, Sir E. H., Bart.
Carling, Mr. F. R., J.P. (2)
Carling, Mr. W. R.
Carter, Mr. C. (3)
Chancellor, Mr. A., M.S.A.
Chaplin, Mr. J.
Chapman, Mr. A. W., J.P.
Chapman, Mr. T.
Chester, Mr. H. M.
Chilton, Captain A. R. T.
Chitty, Mr. George
Clarke, Mr. J.

Clemence, Mr. T. R.
Clephane, General A. R.
Clinton, Mr. A. G.
Cole, Mr. W.
Coles, Mrs.
Collier, Mr. J. C., J.P.
Cooke, Mr. H.
Cooke, Mrs. J.
Cooper, Rev. T. S., F.S.A.
Coote, Mr. A.
Conrage, Mrs.
Crooke, Mr. F. A.
Crouch, Mr. E.
Crundwell, Mr. E.
Cullerne, Mr. W. S. V.
Curtis, Mr. A. C.
Curtis, Rev. H. C.
Davey, Mr. E.
Davies, Mr. F. G.
Davies, Rev. G. S.
Day, Mr. A.
Deacon, Mr. W. S.
Denyer, Mr. G. T.
Dewar, Mr. Peter
Du Buisonby, Mr. W. H.
Doulton, Sir Henry
Ellis, Mr. E. C.
Ellis, Mr. Edwin, J.P.
Ellis, Mrs. John
Ellis, Mr. L. A.
Ellis, Mr. Stanley
Emery, Mr. W.
Emery, Mr. W. R.
Few, Mrs.
Filmer, Miss A. H.
Fleet, Mr. W. H.
Folker, Mr. H. S.
Folker, Mr. A. H.
Foster, Mr. Edmund
French, Mr. A. B.
Frost, Miss
Gabb, Dr.
Gammon, Mr. J. F.
Gassiot, Captain
Gaye, Rev. H. C.
Gill, Mr. H. J.
Godman, Mr. J., J.P.
Goodman, Dr. R. N.
Grayling, Mrs. F.
Greir, Miss
Guildford and Working Men's [Institute
Guildhall Library, London, E.C.
(C. Welch, F.S.A., Librarian)
Gunner, Mr. H.

Gyatt, Mr. A.
Hadden, The Misses
Hagart, the late Miss
Haig-Brown, Rev. Canon, D.D.
Haines, Mr. B. J.
Halsey, Mr. E. J., J.P.
Hankin, General G. C., C.B., J.P.
Hart, Rev. J. Beattie
Hayter, Mr. C.
Healey, Mr. E. C., J.P.
Henning, Mr. W. W., J.P.
Hesse, Miss
Hextall, Mr. T.
Heysham, General
Hichens, Mr. A. K.
Hilbers, Dr.
Hodgson, Mr. C. D.
Holden, Mr. C.
Honeybourne, Mr. J. C.
Hooper, Miss M. E.
Hudlestone, Mrs. R.
Hyde, Mr. J. (2)
Jacobs, Mr. G. J.
Jeffery, Mr. S. R.
Jeffries, Mrs. H.
Jekyll, Mrs.
Jekyll, Miss
Jones, Mr. Stanley
Jones, Mr. T. (2)
Jones, Yarrell and Co.
Joynes, Hon. Mrs.
Kingham, Mr. R. D.
King, Mrs.
Knutsford, Right Hon. Lord. G.C.M.G.
Lacy, Mrs.
Lailey, Mr. C. N.
Lamb, Miss
Lasham, Mr. F.
Leach, Mr. J. P.
Leader, Mr. B. W., A.R.A.
Lee, Rev. G. H.
Lee, Mr. W.
Lemare, Mr. F. H.
Leonard, Mr. H. Selfe
Lidderdale, Colonel
Locke-King, Miss E.
Loftus, Mrs.
Longbottom, Mr. D.
Longworth, Mr. W.
Lower, Mr. W. G.
Lunn, Mr. E. L.
Lunn, Mr. H. M.
Macdonald, Mr. D., J.P.

Macnamara, Mr. F. N.
Maitland, Mr. A. W.
Mangles, Mr. H. A.
Mangles, Mr. Ross, V.C.
Marsack, General A. B., J.P.
Martin, Mrs. Waller
Mathew, Mrs.
Mathison, Major
Matthews, Mr. W.
Matthews, Mr. Percy
Maybank, Mr. J. T.
McGaw, Mr. Joseph
Mellersh, Mr. A. W.
Merewether, Colonel G., R.E.
Miles, Mr. Walker'
Miller, Mr. Cecil W.
Molineux, Major J. W.
Montagnue, Lieut.-General A. P.
Moon, Mr. Alfred
Moon, Mr. A. E.
Moore, Captain R., R.N.
Morton, Dr. J.
Moxon, Mr. A. E.
Munro, Captain G. T.
Napper, Mr. H. F.
Napper, Miss R.
Nevill, Mr. R., F.A.S.
Newbold, Mr. R.
Newell, Miss
Newman, Mr. T. P.
Niall, Dr. W. G.
Northcott, Mr. S.
Nye, Mr. R.
Ogilvie, Mr. G. Stuart, J.P.
Oliphant, Rev. F. J.
Onslow, Right Hon. Earl of, G.C.M.G. (2)
Onslow, Miss H.
Onslow, Mr. R.
Oughterson, Mr. G. B.
Page, Mr. H. J.
Page, Mr. T. E. (2)
Palmer, Mr. C. A.
Parker, Mr. A. C.
Patrick, Mr. A. H.
Patrick, Mr. W. T.
Paulton, Mrs.
Peak, Mr. H.
Peake, Mr. J. M., Liphook
Pearson, Mr. C. A.
Penzance, Right Hon. Lord
Perreau, Colonel M. C.
Perryman, Mrs. Wilbraham-
Philpott, Miss M.

Pinun, Mrs. W. A.
Pitman, Captain J. C., R.N.
Pocock, Mr. W. W.
Pontifex, Major W.
Potter, Mr. H.
Powell, Mr. T. W.
Powell, Mrs.
Powell, Mrs., Hampton Wick
Powell, Miss
Puckle, Mrs.
Pullman, Mr. E. E.
Ramsden, Mr. J. C., J.P.
Randall, Mr. G.
Rea, Mr. T., J.P.
Rees, Mr. Thos.
Reynard, Mr. J. L. A.
Ricardo, Colonel H., J.P.
Rich, Sir Charles H. Stuart, Bart., F.S.A.
Robinson, Miss
Romanis, Rev. W. F. J.
Rosebery, Right Hon. Earl of, K.G.
Rowcliffe, Mr. E. L., J.P.
Rowe, Mr. E. R. F., J.P. (2)
Russell, Lady Arthur
Russell, Mr. Harold
Ryde, Mr. E. H.
Sadler, Mr. J.
Salsbury, Mr. R. (Mayor of Guildford)
Salvin, Captain F. H.
Sandwith, Colonel
Savage, Mr. W. H.
Schollick, Mr. T. J.
Scott, Mr. C. J.
Shackell, Edwards and Co., Messrs.
Shawcross, Mr. W.
Shepherd, Mr. G. P.
Sheppard, Mr. H.
Simmonds, Mr. J. W.
Simpson, Mr. J.
Simpson, Mr. R. T.
Skelton, Mrs. H.
Sligo, Marchioness of
Smallpeice, Mr. F.
Smallpeice, Mr. M.
Smith, Colonel Graham
Smith, Mr. Henry (2)
Snoxell, Mr. S.
Sparkes, Mr. R.
Stedman, Mr. R. B. (3)
Stephenson, Mr. Mill
Stevens, Mr. Wm.
Stevenson, Major W.

Storey, Mr. W. C.
Storr, Mr. Rayner
Street, Mr. W.
Sturges, Mr. H. H.
Sturt, Mr. W. E.
Surrey, the Right Hon. Lord-Lieutenant of
Sutcliff, Dr. J. H.
Swaine, Mrs.
Swayne, Mr. Wm., J.P.
Swayne, Miss
Tayler, Mr. G., J.P. (2)
Taylor, Mr. J. T.
Temple, Rev. R.
Templeman, Mr.
Thomas, Mr. C.
Trench, Mr. W. P.
Trenchard, Mr. C. E. Dillon
Tucker, Mr. T.
Tyler, Mr. Chas. T.
Unwin, Mr. G.
Valpy, Rev. Canon A. S.
Vertue, Miss
Vickridge, Mr. A. H. (2)
Vickers, Mr. E. J.
Wakefield, Dr. Horace
Waterfield, Mrs. Wyndham
Watts, Mr. G. F., R.A.
Watts, Mrs. G. F.
Webb, Mr. E.
Welch, Mr. W.
Wells, Mr. W., J.P.
Welman, Mr. S.
Wenham, Miss
Weston, Colonel, J.P.
Wheat, Mr. G. C.
Wheeler, Mr. F.
White, Mr. Gilbert H.
Wiles, Mr. J. H.
Wilkinson, Mr. R.
Williamson, Mr. D., J.P.
Williamson, Mr. D., Jun.
Williamson, Mr. F. G.
Williamson, Mr. Martin
Williamson, Mrs. W. (2)
Winchester, Lord Bishop of
Woodhouse, Mr. F. V.
Woolley, Mrs. Chas.
De Worms, Baron H., M.P.
Wrist, Mr. C.
Yool, Mrs. H.
Young, Miss L. M.
Young, Miss E. G.
Younghusband, Mr. J. E.

www.ingramcontent.com/pod-product-compliance
Lightning Source LLC
Chambersburg PA
CBHW030601270326
41927CB00007B/1005